MIXOL

THE JOURNAL OF THE

VOLUME TWO

PUBLISHER

Jared Brown

EDITOR

Anistatia Miller

MANAGING EDITOR

Robert Hess

COPY EDITOR

Joshua E. London

CONTRIBUTORS

Jared Brown, Dale DeGroff, Robert Hess, Ryan Magarian,
Anistatia Miller, Darcy O'Neil, Gary Regan, Audrey Saunders,
Christine Sismondo, LeNell Smothers, Gwydion Stone

MIXELLANY
AN IMPRINT OF
JARED BROWN

MIXOLOGIST

THE JOURNAL OF THE AMERICAN COCKTAIL

Volume Two

COVER DESIGN

Ted Haigh

TEXT DESIGN

Anistatia Miller

Mixologist: The Journal of the American Cocktail is published annually by Mixellany, an imprint of Jared Brown. A portion of net proceeds from the sales of Mixologist benefits the Museum of the American Cocktail, a non-profit 501(c)(3) organization dedicated to the celebration of the American Cocktail's rich history.

All correspondence should be addressed to:
Jared Brown
459 Columbus Avenue, Suite 201
New York NY 10024 USA

Email: mixellany@mac.com

First printing

ISBN: 0-9760937-1-5

CONTENTS

FROM THE EDITOR

BIRTHDAYS ARE ODD BEASTS. After the innocent joys of childhood, birthday parties give way to alcohol-fogged memories of such rites as coming of age. Then comes a sage desire to quietly dismiss the annual revelry with stately denial. Does one really want to admit turning thirty, forty, fifty, sixty? Does one want to acknowledge the inevitable sags and wrinkles? Does one willingly allow the facts of one's personal history to get added up as the years progress? Does one resign themselves to growing old gracefully or resolve to evolve, offering descendants an invaluable legacy?

Well, I for one am pro-evolution and revelry this year as we face three major birthdays. The bicentennial of the word "cocktail" and the sesquicentennials of the words "mixologist" and "*aperitivo*" are landmarks that should not go unattended, uncelebrated, or unmeditated. These are the days to clearly record the histories and take the cocktail to new horizons.

It's a banner era for the cocktail. The US publication *Food & Wine* proclaimed 2005 to be the "Year of the Cocktail," featuring some of the brightest young stars in the cocktail world. The Nineties (and the Naughties) have seen the cocktail elevate itself from the ashes of drinks like Sex on the Beach and the Fuzzy Navel to the culinary eloquence of revived and revised classics like the Sazerac, Sidecar, and Ramos Gin Fizz.

Two hundred years ago, the word "cocktail" was first defined in print. On May 13, 1806, the editor of *The Balance and Columbian Repository*, a small newspaper published in Hudson, New York, replied to a reader's query as to what

4

a "cocktail" was. (He had used the term in a column the previous week.) He replied:

> Cock tail, then is a stimulating liquor, composed of spirits of any kind, sugar, water and bitters it is vulgarly called a bittered sling, and is supposed to be an excellent electioneering potion inasmuch as it renders the heart stout and bold, at the same time that it fuddles the head. It is said also, to be of great use to a democratic candidate: because, a person having swallowed a glass of it, is ready to swallow any thing else.

These days, mixologists and bar chefs are devising creations that go beyond these simple elements: expanding on nineteenth-century tea syrup and infusion recipes; concocting foams and tinctures and bitters that would make any Cordon Bleu chef envious; and pushing the envelope of invention with a reverent bow to the past.

Mixologist. The name of this publication is often misleadingly thought of as a sophisticated, modern-day term for the term "bartender. The truth is, mixologist has been used to define a type of bartender for 150 years. The word first appeared in print in *The Knickerbocker Magazine*: publishing home of American greats such as Washington Irving, James Fenimore Cooper, William Bryant, Nathaniel Hawthorne, and Henry Wadsworth Longfellow. In the sixth installment of the story "The Observations of Mace Sloper", in the June 1856 issue, Mace Sloper is reminded of a conversation overheard in a New Jersey hotel:

The word "cocktail" was first defined in print in this reply to a reader's inquiry in *The Balance and Columbian Repository* on May 13, 1806. (From the collection of Robert Hess.)

> In-comes are always welcome," answered No. II. "The mixologist of tipiculars directoried me to apartment XC,

which, being exceedingly weary, I did uncandelized. Yet if you desire illuminosity——

STRANGER!" cried No. I.: 'hold thar! Don't light a match, for the love of God! I know adzackly what you look like without goin furder. You're five feet 'leven inches high, got gray eyes and a coon-colored vest, short-cropped ha'r and a loose over-coat, nose like a razor handle, and scar over your left eye. That's the stripe!

"How do you cognovit that?" was the amazed reply.

"Cog——thunder!" was the response. "How do I know how you look? Why, who the h—l ever heard of a man's coming to bed in the dark, and calling a bar-keep a mixologist of tipicular fixins, unless he had gray eyes, razor-handled nose, short ha'r, an' a coon-colored vest? Don't light a match stranger on my account. Drummon' lights would be darkness on your face arter such as blaze of language as that. 'Illuminosity' and 'cognovit'! That shows you've got a ca'pet-bag in your hand and a whiskey-bottle in it. Sho!"

Obviously the word "mixologist" was a pretentious term for a bartender or bar-keep in the writer's eyes. Yet, about forty years later, the *Police Gazette* encouraged bartenders nationwide to call themselves mixologists, to soften the blows in the media instigated by temperance supporters. (The publication also ran a weekly cocktail column, presenting recipes from mixologists across the country and even conducted a cocktail competition in 1901.)

Thankfully, mixologists are now accepted as experts in the culinary art of cocktail making: the execution, presentation, and creation of beverages.

Cocktail hour: It's that magic transitional period between the end of work and dinner (usually clocked between 1700 and 1900 hours), when people from all walks of life gather in bars, lounges, and clubs to socialize over cocktails created by mixologists and to savor a few hors d'oeuvres. Invented in the Piedmonte capital of Turin (Torino), *aperitivo*—the ritual cocktail hour—has been observed daily for 150 years at the myriad cafés that cater to all tastes and social strata.

Legend has it that a Torinese bartender invented an aperitivo—the drink—in 1856, just because he wanted to try his hand at making at American-style libation, adding ice, bitters, and a splash of soda water to vermouth (the fortified wine that took the city's café society by storm after Antonio Benedetto Carpano introduced in 1786). When Gaspare Campari added his eponymously-named mild bitters to the Torino-Milano in 1860, the Americano was born. More pre-dinner specialties followed the Negroni, the Elisa, and the Bellini.

Aperitivi are never served alone in Italy. Each drink is accompanied by a signature food pairing, included in the price though never mentioned on the menu. A small plate of *tramezzini* (sandwiches of lobster salad or salmon and row), grilled prosciutto and fontina sandwiches, or small rounds of puff pastry filled with a lightly seasoned tomato paste certainly are more appealing than the offerings of mini pretzels, popcorn, or Swedish meatballs from the steamer tray served during conventional American "happy hours."

Thankfully, the *aperitivo* concept is being revived in a current wave of non-Italian establishments like the Pegu Club in New York, where patrons are offered tuna tartare, mini duck breast sandwiches, and the like, purposefully crafted to accompany cocktails.

These are not a series of quiet birthdays. Gala celebrations are taking place on the cocktail's bicentennial in New York, Las Vegas, London, and Sydney. Cocktail competitions are growing in number and dimension. Our own annual journal will publish two volumes in this landmark year. And this volume's roster of contributors proves that the two-hundred-year-old cocktail is not a stately old dame remembered only for her past. The cocktail is very much a living, vital tradition that continues to evolve as the decades march on.

Thanks and extra olives go to our Managing Editor Robert Hess for reaching out and nurturing some of this volume's articles as well as his own double contribution; to our Copy Editor Joshua E. London for making us readable; and to our contributors Gary Regan, Dale DeGroff, Audrey Saunders, Christine Sismondo, LeNell Smothers, Darcy O'Neil, Gwydion Stone, and Ryan Magarian for sharing their knowledge of the world that is the cocktail.

Anistatia Miller
Editor

OUR CONTRIBUTORS

JARED BROWN & ANISTATIA MILLER

Authors and spirits specialists, Jared Brown and Anistatia Miller drink and write about drinks for a living. Established in 1995, their website *Shaken Not Stirred:® A Celebration of the Martini* led to the publication of the book by the same name (HarperCollins, 1997 and Europa Verlag, 1998). Their homage to the bubbly, *Champagne Cocktails*, was published two years later (ReganBooks, 1999). They are contributing editors for *Hamptons*, *Gotham*, *LA Confidential*, and *Aspen Peak* magazines. Their articles have also appeared in *Wine Spectator*, *Cigar Aficionado*, *FoodArts*, *Slammed*, *Theme*, and *DiffordsGuide to Drinking* (UK).

Their podcast program—"At Brown's Bar"—is broadcast on iTunes and on their web site www.martiniplace.com.

They are founders—along with Dale DeGroff, Robert Hess, and others—of the Museum of the American Cocktail. They are also publishers of Mixellany Books, the museum's publishing arm, which produces the annual *Mixologist: The Journal of the American Cocktail*; Jared Brown serves as its publisher, Anistatia Miller as its editor.

Miller and Brown developed Heavy Water Vodka's formula, which has won six medals including the Beverage Tasting Institute's (BTI's) gold medal in 2005 before it was released in October 2005 and a gold medal at the 2006 San Francisco World Spirits Competition. They also helped to develop gin, rum, and vodka for North America's first micro-distillery restaurant, The Bardenay. (The gin received a BTI score of 92 points at its 2003 tasting.)

They have created signature cocktails for spirits companies, bars, and clubs, and served as brand ambassadors for Martini & Rossi and Bacardi. This husband-and-wife team has made numerous TV and radio appearances, discussing their favorite subjects—cocktails and spirits. They've been quoted in *USA Today*, *The New York Times*, *Santé*, *Cheers*, *Theme* (UK), *MarketWatch*, and *Playboy*. They've taught consumers how to shake and stir their own cocktails at Morton's Steakhouses nationwide, Southern Comfort's Annual Tales of the Cocktail Spirited Dinners; and they've narrated the history of spirits and cocktails for the Culinary Historians of New York, the James Beard Foundation, the Museum of the American Cocktail, and in private group sessions.

DALE DEGROFF

Dale DeGroff is universally acknowledged as the world's premier mixologist. DeGroff developed his extraordinary techniques and talent tending bar for over twenty-five years at great establishments, most notably New York City's famous Rainbow Room, where, from 1987 to 1999, he pioneered a gourmet approach to recreating the great classic cocktails. Referred to as the "King of Cocktails," DeGroff is often credited with reinventing the profession of bartending and setting off a cocktail explosion throughout the world.

Debonair, a great raconteur, and unparalleled authority, his prominence and innovations continue to grow and impact the bar industry. DeGroff provides consulting and bar training to spirits manufacturers and leading restaurants and hotel chains, and serves as director of beverage arts for part of the year at the Halekulani Hotel. Honored with Spirits Professional awards from *Nightclub & Bar*, *Saveur*, *Cheers*, *Santé*, *Food Arts*, and *Bon Appétit* magazines, and also a James Beard award nomination. DeGroff appears regularly in the press and media including: Fine Living Network, Food Network, *Cooks Tour, Simply Ming, B. Smith, Martha Stewart*, CNN, *Today Show*, Discovery Channel, and History Channel. He also writes monthly columns for *Theme* and *Beverage Media*.

This year, DeGroff teamed up with four other spirits professionals in order to launch Beverage Alcohol Resource (BAR), an organization that provides training in mixology. DeGroff is also the founding President of The Museum of the American Cocktail (www.MuseumOfTheAmerican-Cocktail.org), the first museum in the world devoted to the historical study and appreciation of the cocktail. (Its inaugural exhibit was in the heart of the French Quarter in New Orleans, with new exhibits now open in New York and Las Vegas.)

ROBERT HESS

Robert Hess is the managing editor of *Mixologist: The Journal of the American Cocktail*, Hess is also a Director at Microsoft and traces his interest in cocktails to a childhood fascination of bartenders, who effortlessly transformed the contents of the bottles around them into gleaming jewels of refreshment. Eventually he took action on these early memories, absorbing all he could about the classic art of mixology. Using his culinary training as a canvas, he views cocktails as a cuisine with the same artistic flavor potentials as that of any French chef. He has since become a ceaseless evangelist of quality cocktails, working with restaurants, bartenders, and consumers—as well as creating the informative and widely recognized website www.DrinkBoy.com—to increase recognition and respect for this undervalued art. Hess, along with several other notable mixologists, organized and founded The Museum of the American Cocktail.

11

Ryan Magarian

For the past decade, Ryan Magarian's unique "chef like" approach to mixology along with the development of several innovative bar programs has gained him recognition as one of America's top mixologists.

Based in Seattle, Ryan works exclusively with Kathy Casey Food Studios, owned by celebrity chef Kathy Casey. Always pushing for both consistency and innovation, Ryan's unique and distinctive approach to his craft balances creative and richly flavored cocktails, consistent drink production, speed, and well-honed technique. In his years as barman and on the consulting front, he was, in 2002, nominated as Best Bartender in Portland and was named Best Bartender in Seattle. Most recently, he was tapped as Seattle's Best Mixologist by *Seattle Weekly*.

His cocktails have received notice in *The New York Times, Wall Street Journal, Wine Enthusiast,* and *Southwest Spirit. Food & Wine* tapped him as one of America's "fiercest young industry talents" and awarded him a coveted 2004 Tastemaker Award.

Current projects include focused cocktail development, seminars, and bar trainings for Merritt Hospitality, installing a unique "culinary" cocktail program for its properties nationwide, and developing a wide range of luxury spirit brands. He is a spokesperson f or FRIS vodka and develops its signature line of vodka infusions. At the new Suite 410, in downtown Seattle, he is overseeing the development of a vintage cocktail program.

He also developed signature drinks for Restaurants Unlimited, Marriott Hotels, and Holland America Line cruise ships.

Darcy S. O'Neil was born in Sarnia, Ontario and spent many of those years living near the beach. A cold Canadian beach, but a beach none-the-less. After high school, the decision of a career choice was whittled down to chemistry or the culinary arts. With a little thought, chemistry was the choice. At the time, it seemed logical that laboratory skills were more transferable to the kitchen than cooking skills to the lab. Four years later, he received his diploma in chemistry.

After a six-year stint working in a world-class oil and gas research facility, the time for change arrived, via a downsizing notice. After a couple of false starts in the pharmaceutical and information technology worlds, the possibility of going to chef school returned. During a period of quiet contemplation, and a few drinks, he was whacked with the epiphany stick and the marriage of chemistry and bartending dawned upon him.

With a little research into the world of mixology and a completely stocked home bar, that rivaled many professional bars, and irritated his wife with all the clutter, the fusion of science and art began. As he rifled through the classic drinks, to modern interpretations, and the occasional vile concoction, the chemistry skills started to refine the art. A whole new world of experimental flavors opened up in a way that satisfied his experimental curiosity and his culinary cravings. A bartender was born.

Currently, Darcy is employed as a bartender and introducing people to great cocktails. He can also be found writing about original cocktail creations and other bartender related topics at www.theartofdrink.com.

Gary Regan

Gary Regan is a bartender/writer who writes a cocktail column for *The San Francisco Chronicle*, and is published in a variety of magazines including *The Wine Enthusiast*, *Gourmet*, and *Cheers*. He teaches professional bartender classes in his hometown of Cornwall-on-Hudson, New York, and along with his wife, Mardee Haidin Regan, he co-hosts a web site at www.ardentspirits.com, and publishes an e-mail newsletter, *Ardent Spirits*. Gary tended bar for many years in Manhattan, and still pulls an occasional shift at his local inn.

Audrey Saunders

Audrey Saunders opened The Pegu Club in New York City's Soho district, in the summer of 2005. Originally a British officers club in Rangoon, her intention in resurrecting the Pegu Club was to preserve a part of old-world cocktail culture through thoughtful preparation and respectful methodology. The original club was infamous for its house cocktail—the Pegu Cocktail itself is an old, gin-based classic that is unabashedly indicative of exactly the sort of drinking culture that she wishes to pay homage to. Her goal is that the reestablishment of the Pegu Club will serve as a beacon to those who hold the craft of the cocktail in high esteem, as well as a Shangri-La to all of the new friends who first enter.

Early in her career, she attended night classes at the Institute of Culinary Education to expand her basic foundation for the blending of flavors and densities, for as most Michelin-starred chefs would agree, gastronomic perfection is found in the details. Though precise proportions and methods are less of a concern behind most bars, Saunders is a perfectionist and has been known to re-mix possible new recipes forty or fifty times during the creation process—before finally pinpointing the perfect components and measures for her recipes.

Saunders' story behind the bar begins in 1996 when she was working concurrently in Brooklyn Heights at The Waterfront Ale House. The manager knew of her interest in cocktail creation, and suggested that she take a seminar at New York University that was being offered by Master Mixologist Dale DeGroff. After finishing the seminar, Saunders was so enthralled that she approached DeGroff, offering to work for free in exchange for training. By 1997, she became involved with DeGroff for special events for the Rainbow Room, such as an evening making drinks for the Mayor at Gracie Mansion.

In 1999, she and DeGroff opened Blackbird on East 49th Street where they worked side by side, and Saunders painstakingly proved herself to regulars by mixing DeGroff's specialties to perfection. After Blackbird, she furthered her skills by taking on positions as Bar Manager at Beacon Restaurant (Blackbird's sister restaurant), and then as Beverage Director of The Tonic Restaurant.

Audrey joined The Carlyle in February, 2002 for the much-acclaimed reopening of New York's legendary Bemelmans Bar. She spent her tenure there creating, developing and fine-tuning a beverage program which has earned The Carlyle a global reputation for cocktails; *Forbes Magazine* voting it one of the top 20 bars in the world. She shared a lot of her time between New York and London, spending Thanksgiving holidays as a guest mixologist at The Ritz hotel in London, and working closely with their staff. During her stays in the UK, she also appeared on BBC television, BBC radio, conducted cocktail seminars at Milk & Honey, and has judged cocktail competitions. She has been written about internationally, appearing in such publications as *The New York Times*, *The London Times*, *The Financial*

Times, BusinessWeek, Wall Street Journal, Forbes, Tatler, Esquire, The Observer, The Guardian, The Caterer, New York Magazine, Town & Country, Gentleman's Quarterly, Wine Enthusiast, Wine & Spirits, Bon Appétit, FoodArts, Food & Wine, Glamour, and *InStyle Magazine.* Her menu at Bemelmans Bar features truly unique cocktails, which include a number of her original creations as well as old world classics.

Audrey is also the beverage co-chair for NYC chapter of City-Meals-On-Wheels, and Share Our Strength/Taste of the Nation charities. She is also a supporter of the Museum of the American Cocktail.

Christine Sismondo

Christine Sismondo calls herself a slackademic, meaning that the entire time she entertains youth in the university lecture hall is generally spent wishing she were working on the history of cocktails and the social history of vice in general. Fortunately, she managed to take a year off recently to write and publish *Mondo Cocktail: A Shaken and Stirred History*, so all her dreams are pretty much fulfilled. She is also senior editor of a magazine about academic life, a frequent book reviewer and, until recently maintained a once a week job bartending. Now retired from that, she is content to tend her home bar.

LeNell Smothers

LeNell Smothers is the president of LeNell's Ltd, a Wine & Spirit Boutique, located in New York City. After drinking too much and staying up a few nights to watch the sun rise while contemplating life's journey, she decided to pursue her passion in the arts of cocktailian ways full-time. Despite her degrees in French and Public Administration, she sold her mini-mansion in Alabama and moved to New York City to be close to the heart of cocktail culture and to be an evangelist for bourbon, the official American spirit. She now runs a liquor store that has been touted by New York magazine as the best liquor store in New York City and rated in the "Top Ten" shops in the US by GQ magazine. LeNell's Ltd has been highlighted in publications such as *The New York Times, New York Sun, New York Post,* and *Absolute* magazine. She is also a full-time preacher of the gospel of American whiskey to bars, restaurants, and consumers.

GWYDION STONE

Gwydion Stone has long been intrigued by obscure and arcane subjects. It was only natural that, when he first encountered the notorious green spirit known as absinthe, he should try to get to the bottom of its romance, allure, and mystique. He soon learned that most information available was misleading, inaccurate, or just plain fraudulent. This prompted his journey toward discovering the truth behind the "Green Fairy," and gaining a deeper understanding of what it was, and was not. He now runs the Wormwood Society, a sort of "absinthe anti-defamation" organization, as well as one of the web's most respected and fastest growing discussion forums for absinthe aficionados, www.WormwoodSociety. org. Stone is constantly working at dispelling the myths and misconceptions surrounding this drink.

A truly American cocktail, the mint julep has a long and distinguished history. (Photo by Jared Brown.)

CLASSIC COCKTAILS

On the 200th anniversary of the cocktail, what's more fitting than to start this edition of Mixologist: The Journal of the American Cocktail with an in-depth look at the significance of the cocktail in the historical records, the story of the Mint Julep, a distinguished predecessor to the libation that contains "spirits of any kind, bitters, sugar, and water," and the origin of the most notorious concoction to grace a cocktail glass in the late twentieth century.

THE COCKTAIL

THE FIRST AMENDMENT
AND THE PROFESSIONALIZATION
OF THE INDUSTRY

BY CHRISTINE SISMONDO

The word has existed for two centuries. But what's really behind the term "cocktail"? Christine Sismondo explores the word's politically-charged, often contested origins, evolution, and future.

WHERE DOES THE WORD "cocktail" come from? Two hundred years later, the debate still rages on. Is it possible that the answer has been hiding in plain sight all along?

In "The Vocabulary of the Drinking Chamber", cocktail hero Henry Louis Mencken complains that none of the great reference tools of his day—like *An History of American English* or *The Dictionary of Slang*—attempt to "unravel the mystery of the cocktail."[1] Many attempts have been made since, although no definitive answer has emerged.

Mencken, writing in 1948, outlined the problem with his contemporary competing etymologies. At that point he had collected "forty or fifty" theories and had pronounced nearly all of them "baloney."

We need not list every false origin here. Suffice it to say that Colonel Carter refused to drink up the cock-ale and mixed dregs of kegs in the giant ceramic rooster Betsy Flanagan kept in her henhouse (next to her stable of cocktailed horses) during the revolutionary war, and then everyone put feathers in their drinks to celebrate the victor of the cockfight, owned by none other than the lovely Aztec princess Xochtil.

Mencken's instincts about language were enviable. Or, perhaps we should say that after a lifetime of studying the American language, he had a good sense for how words evolved, and this instinct and expertise led him to doubt the most convincing and accepted theory around, namely, the Peychaud egg cup etymology.

For many years, New Orleans lore asserted the origin of the word to be homegrown. Stanley Clisby Arthur may have been the first to put this theory in print and, when

---

1. H.L. Mencken, "The Vocabulary of the Drinking Chamber," in *Drinking, Smoking and Screwing: Great Writers on Good Times*, ed. by Sara Nickles (San Francisco: Chronicle Books: 1994).

he did, he stated it as fact and gave no sources to back up the Crescent City cocktail claim.

Arthur, in his 1937 *Famous New Orleans Drinks and How to Mix 'Em*, stated that Antoine Amedée Peychaud, New Orleans apothecary, served up a very popular brandy-bitters concoction in an egg-cup, known as a *coquetier*, which evolved over time (and much consumption) into our modern word "cocktail" around 1795.

Sounded very plausible. After all, cocktails are as central to New Orleans culture and history as jazz. Indeed, where else should the word cocktail have been invented? It sounded fairly plausible to Mencken, too, although he had some misgivings. And most of these stemmed from the fact that he was well aware the word existed in print as early as May 6, 1806, in the periodical, *The Balance and Columbian Repository*, published in Hudson, New York.

Shortly after an election, there was a cartoon-like editorial alluding to the amount of money the Democratic-Republican candidate spent on alcohol to ply voters, and one of the entries on the itemized list was "25 do. Cocktails." Added to the 720 rum-grogs, 17 brandy, 32 gin-slings and 411 glasses of bitters, this is a pretty healthy bar tab to have incurred, only to then lose the election.[2]

About a week later, a clever reader who shall be referred to as the "Subscriber"—and clearly no Democratic-Republican, either—wrote to the editor to congratulate him on his political satire and to inquire as to the word "cocktail." He'd not heard of the word, despite a familiarity with the terms "phlegm-cutter and fog driver, of wetting the whistle, of moistening the clay, of a fillip, a spur in the head, quenching a spark in the throat, of flip & c."[3]

---

2. I'm using the reproduction of the article from The Museum of the American Cocktail's website: http://www.museumoftheamericancocktail.org/museum/TheBalance.html.

Now, this Subscriber may have been no Mencken, who had described himself as "ombibulous" (always quick with amusing neologisms) and claimed to have tried 273 cocktails. Mencken also collected hundreds of new words (he called Americanisms) related to drinking, but our eloquent and informed anonymous letter writer has clearly put some time and thought into the vocabulary of the drinking chamber, himself.

Subscriber asks the editor: "Does it signify that the democrats who take the potion are turned topsycurvy, and have their heads where their tails should be?"

The editor of *The Balance* never addresses this fanciful suggestion and offers the following definition in his May 13, 1806, publication:

> Cock tail, then, is a stimulating liquor, composed of spirits of any kind, sugar, water and bitters it is vulgarly called a bittered sling, and is supposed to be an excellent electioneering potion inasmuch as it renders the heart stout and bold, at the same time that it fuddles the head. It is said also, to be of great use to a democratic candidate: because, a person having swallowed a glass of it, is ready to swallow any thing else.[4]

I include the political slurs here—whereas many accounts leave out this aspect—because they have a direct bearing on the word's invention and also foreshadow the rich history of the cocktail and politics—something which we shall explore further in this meditation on the word.

As to the description of the drink itself, many have pointed out, including Mencken, that this seems to be the recipe for an Old Fashioned cocktail and further, that the word cocktail may have at one point referred to that specific drink, rather than its present usage, where it has come to mean an entire class of drinks.

---

3. Ibid.
4. Ibid.

That, in itself, is an interesting philological (the study of linguistic change over time) development, in that it indicates the term became so popular that it squeezed out bittered sling, phlegm-cutter, fog-driver and spur in the head—all seemingly excellent names—as the most fitting word to describe the class of beverage made from potent liquors and the activity of drinking them over the last 200 years.

In 1976, Richard Dawkins, British anthropologist, proposed the "meme theory," in which he posited that catchphrases, ideas and other small units of cultural information could reproduce and be passed on through copying—we mimic each other and the meme is replicated—in a similar fashion to the replication of genes.[5]

Strong, popular (although not necessarily correct) units of cultural meaning (memes) would thrive and replicate, even if they are sometimes altered slightly in the copying process like a game of broken telephone. Weak memes die out and become cultural relics. If this theory is correct and the word cocktail can properly be called a meme, the word and idea has been a truly remarkable survivor, proving far more fit than any of the other hundreds of words concocted over the years that have disappeared from popular speech.[6]

Seeing as the drink described in *The Balance* appears to be none other than an Old Fashioned, we can also imagine the origin of the name of that drink. Perhaps in honor of retired civil war Colonel James E. Pepper at the Pendennis Club in Louisville, Kentucky, somebody added some other ingredient like, say, sweet vermouth or pomegranate mo-

---

5. Richard Dawkins, *The Selfish Gene* (London: Oxford University Press, 1990).
6. This theory is not very popular in Kansas where they insist on teaching the alternative theory that cocktail is a word that came about through Intelligent Design.

lasses, or omitted a traditional ingredient, like, say, bitters
and called it a cocktail.[7]

At which point, we can fancifully imagine how somebody might have objected that the new beverage was not, in fact, a proper cocktail which was traditionally made with spirits, sugar, water, and bitters. To which somebody might have responded that this objection was based on a rather pedantic usage of the word. The Old Fashioned, then, would have become the traditional Platonic ideal of what evolved into an entire genre of drinks.

Or perhaps not. The point of our little imaginary etymological shift is simply that this is how a meme, when copied, can change subtly and come to mean an entirely new thing altogether.

But back to our competing etymologies. Mencken's reservations about the Peychaud story are clearly outlined in his 1948 essay. Aside from noting that Stanley Clisby Arthur has no sources to back up his story, Mencken mentions this more puzzling problem: "How did Peychaud's invention, if it was his invention, make its way from New Orleans to so remote a place as Hudson, New York, in so short a time, and how did it become so generalized on the way?"[8]

This, in itself, would not have dissuaded me from believing in the very compelling Peychaud story. After all, with what we now know about memes, a very popular meme such as the word "cocktail" could have traveled far and wide. Drinks travel fast. Even faster are the words we use to describe them.

---

7. This is one theory about the invention of the Old Fashioned. This event took place prior to 1895, and I am indebted to Robert Hess for this story.

8. H.L. Mencken, "The Vocabulary of the Drinking Chamber," in *Drinking, Smoking and Screwing: Great Writers on Good Times*, ed. by Sara Nickles (San Francisco: Chronicle Books: 1994).

However, since Phil Greene, Peychaud descendent and New Orleans historian, published his devastating research into the Peychaud claim last year in the first volume of *Mixologist: The Journal of the American Cocktail* we have a definitive answer that the New Orleans origin story is a fiction. A.A. Peychaud, it seems, would not have been old enough to concoct the city's first Sazerac in 1795 or, indeed, any time before the 1806 mention.[9] Was the story a fiction of Arthur's? Or was it merely an oft-repeated urban legend? We, in all likelihood, will never know. What we can say is that it was a story we wanted to believe and an extraordinarily powerful meme, and memes, you'll recall, are not always correct. Misinformation can travel well, too. That phenomenon is worth studying—urban legends and successful incorrect memes often capture the spirit of the subject matter in a way that archival research doesn't always. We wanted to believe in the Peychaud story because, to an extent, it captured the spirit of the history of the word cocktail.

Even Mencken wanted to believe it. But after relating the story in "The Vocabulary of the Drinking Chamber," he suggests what ultimately turns out to be the correct history: that the word was in use long before Peychaud was shaking up his Sazeracs in the French Quarter.

As for the academic history—the verifiable history— none of this clears up the "mystery" of the word cocktail, unless we simply choose to believe that the editor of *The Balance* made it up, it has been hiding "in plain sight" this whole time and the Peychaud misinformation was what fuddled our minds about the original author. This is my radical suggestion, which I put forth for my fellow cocktail researchers' consideration: that the editor of the Hudson,

---

9. Phil Greene. "Antoine Amedée Peychaud," in *Mixologist: The Journal of the American Cocktail*, volume 1 (New York: Mixellany, 2005), 113-146.

New York periodical invented the neologism himself to
make a larger political point.

This theory is impossible to verify with any certainty. Indeed, we would be challenged with the daunting task of proving that nobody used the word colloquially or otherwise. It is entirely possible that in the barrooms of Hudson folks were in the habit of calling their bittered slings "cocktails," and that the editor simply faithfully recorded his contemporary slang.

Those readers, however, who have ever written on trends will know that as many trends are birthed at an editor's desk as are organically grown and then described by writers (soju cocktails, anyone?). And, at this point, it seems relatively unlikely that, with all the scouring of archival text, we are ever going to find an earlier reference to the word in print.

I submit, then, for several reasons, that the editor made up the word himself.

Let's begin with the editor's identity. Who is the man who first put the word cocktail in print and, furthermore, may very well have invented it? Interestingly, few people have explored this aspect of the mystery and are content to leave the best candidate we have for the inventor of the cocktail nameless. But the author was, almost certainly, one Harry Croswell, a precocious young man who was the sole owner and editor of *The Balance* in Hudson, New York. [10]

Croswell would eventually move to New Haven, Connecticut, and become a minister of the Episcopalian church. He was, by some accounts, very actively involved in trying to help his African-American parishioners become fully integrated into his community and aided in their efforts to establish an African-American church of their own. W.E.B.

---

10. Croswell had partners earlier on in his publishing ventures but became sole owner in 1804.

DuBois, however, called Croswell a reactionary, who was openly opposed to abolition and labeled his attempts to help found an African American Episcopalian church an attempt to institute segregation.[11] But Croswell's controversial work in New Haven only began after his career in journalism was curtailed by a landmark case, which helped to define boundaries involving the freedom of the press.

The Balance, we might guess from the couple of excerpts printed here, was a rather partisan newspaper. Croswell had some fairly strong (negative) opinions about the direction the government was headed in under Thomas Jefferson. Many media historians, in fact, point to Croswell and one of his competitors named Charles Holt as the very first in a long line of partisan media newspapers.

Until that point, newspapers were no less outspoken regarding issues and events but rarely supported a party line wholly or, conversely, attacked the opposing party and its candidates consistently. Croswell was a Federalist; Holt was a staunch Democratic-Republican.[12]

Holt, if you'll bear with us through this little digression, had been publishing a little newspaper called *The Bee* in New London, Connecticut, which had a firmly Democratic-Republican slant and, unlike most political publications today (we hear), very little advertising revenue.

So, the Republican party in Hudson made Holt an offer to come set up shop in their town, move the paper, and be the party's spokesman. Jeffrey L. Pasley, author of *The Tyranny of Printers: Newspaper Politics in the Early American Republic*, notes that at this turning point in the history of

---

11. W.E.B. DuBois, *The Autobiography of W.E.B. DuBois: A Soliloquy on Viewing My Life from the Last Decade of Its First Century* (New York: International Publishers, 1968).

12. Jeffrey L. Pasley, *The Tyranny of Printers: Newspaper Politics in the Early American Republic* (Charlottesville: University of Virginia Press: 2001), 132-152; available online as a sample chapter (#6), at http://pasleybrothers.com/jeff/writings/Chapter%2006,%20Charles%20Holt.htm.

journalism, the *Bee* morphed into an explicit mouthpiece for the Democratic-Republican party. Pasley cites this period as a definitive symbolic and literal moment in the rise of newspaper politics.[13]

Croswell reacted swiftly to the news of Holt's coming newspaper and, by the time *The Bee* began production in the "Democratic Office," located on the second floor of a Hudson building owned by a Democratic-Republican judge, he had already started publishing *The Wasp*, Hudson's Federalist answer to a Republican paper. As Pasley tells us:

> Invoking the image of a larger and more vicious insect able to counteract the invasive species from New London, this was a newspaper devoted entirely to insulting Republicans, with special attention paid to Thomas Jefferson but even more to Charles Holt and other Republican editors in neighboring towns. "Jacobin printers" were being "<u>bought</u> or <u>hired</u>, and set to work in their favorite trade of detraction," Croswell wrote, and it was his job to chastise them. [14]

Clearly, Croswell was dedicated to his cause, but his dedication and political invective would eventually be his downfall. He was charged with sedition in 1802 for his editorials about Jefferson in *The Wasp*. We should mention a couple of facts here for the fact-minded (as Kingsley Amis would say). Jefferson didn't like Croswell's criticisms and used his influence to have him charged with sedition, so he couldn't really be called a very good freedom of speech hero. Although Jefferson was very popular for having rightly repealed the whiskey excise tax and the Louisiana Purchase, he was a wine lover, so not a very good cocktail hero either.

Alexander Hamilton would defend Croswell's right to criticize the government in a groundbreaking First Amend-

---

13. Ibid.
14. Ibid.

ment case. Hamilton's defense (in Croswell's appeal) was that truth should be a defense in libel and sedition cases. Although he could not secure Croswell a new trial, his prosecutors were sympathetic and decided not to seek further judgment. Further, Hamilton's argument was influential in that it proving "truth" would eventually be adopted as a standard for judging the merit of libel cases.[15] Croswell attacked many Democratic-Republicans, including Aaron Burr, who would eventually kill Hamilton in a duel.

One last fact: Croswell's Federalist friends were severely outmatched and quickly fading into cultural relics. The 1800 election had been close for a variety of convoluted reasons to do with the Electoral College; Jefferson nearly lost the office to his running mate, Burr, and wasn't declared victor until February of 1801. The 1804 election, which Jefferson ran with the safer, very popular and apparently more trustworthy George Clinton (who, unlike Burr, wouldn't try to steal the office out from under him), was a landslide for Jefferson.

Burr was nobody's favorite, it seems. Although some Federalists adopted him as a strategic opposition to Jefferson's ascendancy for a while, the cynical gesture was ultimately futile, as even some of the most vehement Jefferson opponents—including Alexander Hamilton—eventually voted his way on the grounds that Burr was so despicable. Hamilton justified his support by claiming that Jefferson was a far less dangerous man.

Burr tried for the New York State governor's office and was successfully blocked by Clinton's political powerhouse. Shortly thereafter, Hamilton was in his cups at some dinner and delivered a "despicable" opinion of Burr in front of a

---

15. Robert W.T. Martin, "Reforming Republicanism: Alexander Hamilton's Theory of Republican Citizenship and Press Liberty," *Journal of the Early Republic* 25 (2005), 21-46.

man named Charles D. Cooper who published this in a letter to the *Albany Register*. What the specific attack was, well, nobody knows. Gore Vidal once famously suggested that Hamilton accused Burr of having an incestuous affair with his daughter but this is almost certainly wrong. The mystery of the insult, like the origin of the word cocktail, is probably lost forever.

At any rate, the duel was on. And we know how that turned out. But before that, Hamilton had vehemently defended Croswell against Jefferson's trumped up sedition charges and claimed that *The Wasp* should not be restricted on account of the need for a freedom of the press. Although eloquent, Hamilton was ultimately unsuccessful—politicians, apparently, were actually far less thick-skinned at the time. This is evidenced by the famous duel, even. Or as Joanne B. Freeman, a Yale historian, explains: "They were men of public duty and private ambition who identified so closely with their public roles that they often could not distinguish between their identity as gentlemen and their status as political leaders."[16]

Hence, publishing vitriolic passages about your opponents having attempted to buy an election with booze (even though that was common practice) and failed, is a potentially more damaging line to take than we might imagine. In a time when we regularly see political leaders abused for the curvature of their private parts, drunken daughters, inability to spell potato or other general buffoonery, it is hard to conceive of the political landmine publishing must have been at the time Croswell was writing. In the intervening eleven years before he decided to give up publishing and Federalist politics, Croswell likely had to tone down his editorial line. Having lost his case

---

16. Joanne B. Freeman, "Dueling as Politics: Reinterpreting the Burr-Hamilton Duel," *William and Mary Quarterly* 53 (1996), 289-318.

for freedom of the press when Hamilton was eloquently defending him, what chance would he have now that his ally had been shot by Burr?

Which leaves me wondering, just who is this Subscriber who asks Croswell to expand on the term "cocktail"? Who is our anonymous man who wrote so eloquently on the vocabulary of the drinking chamber and then suggested that:

> A few years ago, when the democrats were bawling for Jefferson and Clinton, one of the polls was held in the city of New York at a place where ice cream was sold...Something was necessary to cool them. Now when they are sunk into rigidity, it might be equally necessary, by cock-tail to warm and rouse them.

It may very well be that an eloquent and vitriolic reader—in line with Croswell's politics—wrote this letter suggesting the current administration was complacent and listless. We're sure there were plenty such readers. I, however, find the letter slightly suspect, but again, proving authorship here would be next to impossible and perhaps beside the point. What is important is that Croswell chose to publish the reader's letter, to underline the notion that a cocktail was explicitly a political insult. And this is an aspect of the etymology of the word, which is never fully explored.

It is no surprise that cocktails should be tied in with politics. Indeed, in America, booze and voting used to be two peas in a pod. Lender and Martin detail the rich history of the two in their book, *Drinking in America*:

> In the South, politics and drink combined to give the regional vocabulary a new verb, "to treat." One did not seek office at any level without "treating" the electorate during the cam-

paign—that is, without providing all the sundry with generous libations. Polling places themselves were rarely dry.[17]

Lender and Martin go on to point out that all the founding fathers had to have provided beverage in order to get elected, including Thomas Jefferson and George Washington. Of course, we know Washington's liquor bill—it is often cited in debates about campaign finance reform. In his 1757 winning bid for representation in the Virginia House of Burgesses, Washington provided 160 gallons of rum, wine and beer on voting day to voters. What's astounding about that figure is the number of registered voters: only 391.

Not everybody agreed that liquor was an appropriate way to secure votes. Twenty years later, James Madison, running for the same office that Washington had held, refused to supply the electorate their tipple. He never made it to the House. This may be an element of Croswell's point. Our Republican candidate bought many cocktails and gained nothing. Croswell may also be celebrating his fellow citizens' independence and intellect, in that all the campaign money and booze had not bought a bad candidate political office.

Nevertheless, it seems safe to say that the larger critique was about the hypocrisy of the administration. And Croswell would have been particularly piqued at this hypocrisy, having been a victim of it. Key to the Jeffersonian Republican "revolution" of 1800 was a commitment to the freedom of the press. Jefferson, himself, had fought bitterly for this freedom, but once in office, immediately proceeded to curtail the freedom of the press in order to silence Croswell's criticisms.[18]

---

17. Mark Edward Lender and James Kirby Martin, *Drinking in America: A History* (New York: The Free Press, 1987).

18. Robert W.T. Martin, *The Free and Open Press: The Founding of Democratic Press Liberty, 1640–1800* (New York: New York University Press, 2001).

And the word "cocktail," I'd like to speculate, is a word Croswell made up for the purpose of attacking the process. I'm also clearly suspicious of the convenient letter from Subscriber that follows, in which all of the most vehement anti-Republican criticism is launched (in the voice of an independent and impartial reader).

Now, it may very well be that Croswell had the good fortune to have heard somebody use the term "cocktail" in recent days, used it in *The Balance* and then had the good fortune to have a like-minded reader inquire about the word and take it up in precisely the fashion of political insult in which it was meant, allowing the editor to draw out the gag one more week and elaborate further.

But, I submit that it's at least as likely that a litigation-fearing newspaper editor, still bitter about Democratic-Republican interference in the freedom of the press, took to the habit of writing a few of his own letters to the editor. In fact, we know that Croswell, perhaps fearing further recrimination, sometimes published his opinions under a pseudonym. He used "Robert Rusticoat, Esq." as a pen name, under which he wrote in The Wasp.

Posing the debate in the form of a dialectic, after all, is an excellent rhetorical device, and allows our editor to draw out his critique of politicking—after having swallowed a glass of a cocktail, "is ready to swallow anything else."

A brief look at Cornell University's "Making of America" archive confirms that the word was used in a political context for some time. This search, which may not be an exhaustive perusal of American periodicals of the ninenteenth century does at least, we hope, provide a representative sampling of the word cocktail's usage over the hundred or so years before it changed meaning again.

There are a few references to cocktails abroad, which consistently re-confirm the notion that they were perceived as uniquely and consistently American in character and support the notion of a unique and innovative American-style bar being exported as a cultural commodity. At the Vienna Expo in 1893, Clarence Clough Buel describes the *"Amerikanische"* bar at which *"Amerikanische"* cocktails are served.[19] Prior to that, we have an item in the Editor's Drawer of *Harper's New Monthly Magazine* of April 1868:

> The great subject of alcoholic minglings is one that has occupied the mind of the American citizen in every walk of life. Alas! That this should have been thus! The peoples of other nationalities, however, are fast emulating us in this regard, and look with kindly as well as wondering eye on the bibulous triumphs of the Federal saloonist.[20]

This contemplative quote about the nature of "alcoholic minglings" is the *Harper's* editor's pre-amble to the dispatch from the Paris Exposition by Brit, George Augustus Sala, and most specifically his description of the American bar:

At the bar, and from siphon tubes decorated with silvery figures of the American Eagle, were dispensed the delicious 'cream soda' so highly recommended by the faculty; 'cobblers,' 'noggs,' 'smashes,' 'cocktails,' 'eye-openers,' 'mustache-twisters,' and 'corpse-revivers,' were also on hand.[21]

Well, this uniquely American identity is important in that it likely puts to rest the notion that the word was a foreign import—particularly the etymologies which shift the origin to France. No, had cocktail come from the phrase queue de coq or any other such nonsense, there would have surely been protest in 1867. But during this century, the American word seemed to have several distinct associations, which it no longer necessarily has.

---

19. Clarence Clough Buel, "Columbian Exposition: Preliminary Glimpses of the Fair," *The Century* 45 (1893): 622.

20. "Editor's Drawer," *Harper's New Monthly Magazine* 36 (1868), 673.

21. Ibid.

First, we have an undeniable association with cocktails as a breakfast drink. This can be inferred from the names of some of the drinks at the Paris Expo, like the corpse-reviver and the eye-opener. There is very little question now, thanks to the research efforts of William Grimes, Ted Haigh and Gary and Mardee Haidin Regan, that the Corpse-Reviver was a morning drink and remained so well into the twentieth century. The Regans cite Harry Craddock (author of the *Savoy Cocktail Book*) who advised that the drink should be "taken before 11 A.M., or whenever steam and energy are needed."[22]

Of the many references to the word "cocktail" to be found in the Making of America archive, a stunning number of them refer to breakfast, as in, J.W. DeForest's 1871 observation in *The Galaxy* that a particular southerner had "the breath of an 'ante-breakfast' cocktail."[23] Or Wesley Brooke's speculation that "possibly an extra cocktail or two that morning was responsible for the young man's temerity" in an October 1897, issue of *New England Magazine*, when describing a bold southern journalist.[24] Albert Rhodes critiques modern American manners and mores as the average man will "insist on a cocktail before dinner and possibly one before breakfast" in *The Galaxy* in November 1876.[25]

As we've already seen, there is a special association with the south in many early references to cocktails, seen, for example, in this anonymous critique of the typical Virginia editor in *Harper's New Monthly Magazine* in December 1856: "His first waking moments in the morning

---

22. Gary and Mardee Haidin Regan, "Bringing Corpse Revivers to Life," *Ardent Spirits* on Amazon.com. The Regans also quote Craddock's hilarious observation that, "Four of these taken in swift succession will unrevive the corpse again."
23. J.W. DeForest, "Captain Horsfall's Romance," *The Galaxy* 12 (1871): 788-804.
24. Charles Kemble Eichler, "A Pet of the Gods: A Story," *The New England Magazine* 23 (1897): 245-251.

are saturated with a number of powerful cocktails, to cure a headache, 'brought over,' as an accountant would say, from the previous midnight. Cocktailed past the point of nervousness and remorse, he dressed himself, and wends his way to a barber's shop to get shaved..."[26]

This last passage is of particular interest for its colloquial playfulness in transforming cocktail into a verb. I wonder why that usage never became a popular and copied meme? "We got a little cocktailed last night" is certainly an improvement on we got drunk, loaded, plastered or any of the other commonly used terms.

More examples of slurs against southern drinkers can easily be found and, perhaps because of the julep's prominence in American culture, Kentucky is a frequent target. We find Henry Watterson writing in *The Century* in April 1882, in an article called "Oddities of Southern Life," of the typical southerner "who wore a broad-brimmed Panama hat and a great watch fob, who was an expert in the decoction and disposition of mixed liquors."[27] Furthermore, Watterson wrote that the southerner's "morning meal was a simple Kentucky breakfast—three cocktails and a chaw of terbacker."

And occasionally, when Southern gentlemen felt particularly affronted by the insinuation that they engaged in too much cocktailing, they bit back with irreverent wit, like the Kentucky Congressman who was asked why he took two cocktails before breakfast: "One makes me feel like another fellow, and then I must treat the other fellow!"[28]

When describing the famous Paris Expo, Sala indicates that many of these drinks are to be taken in the morning. He mentions the "exhilarating 'morning glory'" and some-

---

26. "Virginian Editor," *Harper's New Monthly Magazine* 14 (1856): 66.
27. Henry Watterson, "Oddities of Southern Life," *The Century* 23 (1886): 884.
28. Hon. S.S. Cox, "Legislative Humors," *Harpers New Monthly Magazine* 52 (1878): 121.

thing surely lost forever to history: "one of them things." He claims that he once had "two of them things" and was so hungover the following day he had to cure it with a hair of the dog which he calls "one of them other things."

This passage, with the many varietals, indicates that cocktails, despite the fact that Croswell described the word as a category of drinks, was commonly used as only one of many terms used to describe a "combination of diverse elements, especially one considered potent."[29] It was far from the universal signifier the word is now.

Using the binomial system of classification as an allegory, in the bibulous kingdom, there is presently the following taxonomy: In the family cocktail, there is a genus of drinks, corpse-revivers, which can then be divided up into species—an example of which is the delicious Corpse-Reviver #2 (*corpsus revivus delectus*).[30] At the time Sala wrote, the word "cocktail" had not yet transcended into an uber symbol for all these mixed drinks—not a family yet, it was merely a genus at the time.

If this evolution is slightly unclear, it might be easy to visualize if we compare it to a linguistic shift that we are currently witnessing. Much to every traditionalist's horror, today's youth and thousands of guilty bar managers across North America now refer to just about any old concoction thrown in a cone-shaped glass with a stem as a "Martini."

Will the word martini displace the word cocktail eventually? Well, not if us old stalwarts have anything to say about it. In my book (and I'm sure to many readers), martinis are still made with gin and remarkably little else. Part of our challenge with the upcoming celebration of the word cocktail in 2006 should be to hold on to it and resist

---

29. As the Oxford English Dictionary now describes it.
30. See the Wile E. Coyote cartoons.

any degradation in language that might lead to the word martini replacing our iconic "cocktail."

Cocktails meant far more than simply a Breakfast of Champions for southerners. The political associations, in keeping with its original usage in *The Balance*, would cling to the cocktail for about a century.

We see this association clearly drawn in a political cartoon in *Harper's* in April 1856:[31]

THE POLITICAL FOOL.
Mr. COCKTAIL BLOATER works for his Party.

The test reads "THE POLITICAL FOOL. Mr. COCKTAIL BLOATER works for his Party." (From the collection of Christine Sismondo.)

And the cocktail crops up repeatedly in descriptions of politicking and lobbying in Washington, as in this passage, again from a *Harper's* article. This excerpt is from February 1867, and called "New York to Washington," in which a politician is described as such: "The Honorable Samuel Janker suggests a cocktail as a preliminary to all conversation…"[32]

Acquaintances in the Southwest (Texas in this case) are accused of discussing politics over "slings and cocktails,"[33]

31. "Foolish Folks-All Fool's Day Sketches," *Harper's New Monthly Magazine* 12 (1856): 717.

32. Arthur Fleming, "New York to Washington," *Harper's New Monthly Magazine* 34 (1867): 367-370.

33. "Some Impressions of London Social Life," by E.S. Nadal. *The Atlantic Monthly* (April 1873): 462-470.

and Albert Rhodes (again) accuses apparent enemies who seem opposed on the house floor of later clinking glasses over oyster stew at the restaurant below. What's in their clinking glasses? Why "whisky-cocktails", of course.[34] And, according to J. Ross Browne, in Sacramento, "during the sittings of the Legislature, measures of the most vital importance are first introduced in rum-cocktails, then steeped in whisky, after which they are engrossed in gin for a third reading."[35]

There are many similar examples. The fact that the word would be used in concert with political slurs so frequently confirms my opinion that, while the word "cocktail" clearly referred to a drink, it also carried a particular political association, namely, that the public had been duped by complacent political bloaters who had become "topsycurvy, and had their heads where their tails should be."

Somehow, along the way, though, the word lost its specifically political insinuation, ceased to be associated with the south predominantly and stopped being a family of morning drinks.

COCKTAILS! NOT JUST FOR BREAKFAST ANYMORE.

The word came to be a universal signifier for mixed concoctions of liquors in glass, with bitters or not. They came to signify more than that, though. The word "cocktail" transcended its early literal associations and evolved into something that began to carry with it certain implications of artistry, luxury, wealth, leisure and even a pinnacle of a gustatory creativity. Some of these changes were starting

---

34. Albert Rhodes, "Speech-Making in Congress," *Scribner's Monthly Magazine* 7 (1874): 297.

35. J. Ross Browne, "Peep at the Washoe," *Harper's New Monthly Magazine* 22 (1861): 150.

to take place in the late 1800s, as saloon-keeping became more professionalized, and cocktail drinking became more stylized during the Gilded Age.

We see the first publication of a cocktail book around this time when, in 1862, Dick and Fitzgerald publish Jerry Thomas' *Bar Tenders Guide*. Thomas provides detailed instructions on general bar maintenance in the opening pages—how to store champagne, handle ice, or pick up fruit with a silver spoon or fork—and he has a clear philosophy outlined as his first bit of advice that, "an efficient bartender's first aim should be to please his customers."

To explain how the word transformed, I suggest we refer back to Dawkins. The word, clearly, was such a successful meme that it quickly edged out all its natural competition: the fog-driver, phlegm-cutter and bittered sling. Or, perhaps, we can put it down to an empowering reclamation of negative terminology. Much as "dyke" and "queer" were reclaimed as positive symbols of identity, their potential as abusive epithets was limited, castrated even. Perhaps some bartender sought to reclaim "cocktail."

Well, maybe not. We'll likely never know the precise reasons for the great shift in the meaning of the word. However, I think we can speculate that, since we can judge roughly when the word began to change, that it had a great deal to do with the professionalization of the bar industry, its export as a cultural commodity to Europe and the fact that the cocktail became more than a vulgarly named bittered sling and a culinary contribution to the gustatory arts in its own right.

Forgive the rather long quote here, but we have tracked down an early instance of the word cocktail's evolution in a story called "A Glimpse of Mexico" from *The Living Age*, dated November 4, 1882. In it, author, F. Francis writes about tippling in Tuscon, being delayed for days on his train trip south:

> Cocktail-drinking has a peculiar charm of its own which lifts it above drinking as otherwise practiced. Your confirmed cocktail-drinker is not to be confused with the ordinary sot. He is a true artist. With what exquisite feeling will he graduate his cups, from the gentle 'smile' of early morn to the potent 'smash' of night. The analytic skill of a chemist marks his swift and unerring detection of the very faintest dissonance in the harmony of the ingredients that compose his beverage. He has an antidote to dispel, a tonic to induce every mood and humor that man knows. Endless variety rewards a single-hearted devotion to cocktails; whilst the refinement and artistic spirit that may be displayed in such an attachment, redeem it from intemperance. It becomes an art. It is drinking etherealized, rescued from vulgar appetite and brutality, purified of its low origin and ennobled. A cocktail hath the soul of wit, it is brief. It is a jest, a bon mot, happy thought, a gibe, a word of sympathy, a tear, an inspiration, a short prayer.

Well, I don't think we could say it any better if we tried.

In fact, this passage sums up all the exquisite associations conjured up by the word cocktail and the cocktail culture that many of us presently aspire to. This is not just a drink, but a cultural icon of civility, luxury and artistry.

And the icon is pervasive and enduring. When we speak of cocktail lounges, parties, dresses or snacks, we are speaking of a highly stylized and refined aesthetic. The cocktail is the couture of the drink world. Nay, couture is the cocktail of the fashion world. Cocktail culture is a distinctly different culture than is found in a frat-house, watering hole or a teenagers' party featuring jungle juice, because, as Francis points out in his passage, a cocktail represents the culmination of a refined and detailed knowledge of spirits and a "harmony of ingredients."

In short, we have Jerry Thomas and his fellow saloon keepers to thank. We owe the transcendence of the cocktail to those dedicated and professional bartenders of days past who elevated the drink and transformed the word from a barb to the sincerest form of praise—the apex of drinking culture.

The professionalization of the industry was not an easy feat to accomplish for our early fore-mixers at the Bank Exchange and the Occidental Hotel. Saloon-keeping, through repressive legislation and common degradation, was a difficult and disreputable profession. That professionalism and artistry was born out of these circumstances make it all the more remarkable.

In a letter to the editor of *The North American Review* in October 1893, arguing for reform in license regulation, Thomas Mador Gilmore states:

> It requires an expert and an array of materials and conveniences to prepare a cocktail, a mint julep, a whiskey sour or any other of the many beverages so delightful to the average palate, and until something better and more convenient offers, the saloon will be retained to fulfill this office.[36]

Over the past hundred years, the cocktail has had its ups and downs. During Prohibition, we know, a good bit of this professionalism was lost. The cocktail then briefly returned to its iconic place, only to be displaced by a generation of wine and micro-brew beers. Palates changed and so did the industry. Aside from sommeliers and a few professionals, the cliché (and all too frequent truth) about bartenders and cocktail waiters were that they were on their way someplace else. Actors, playwrights, and people who couldn't find work in their profession dominated the

---

36. Thomas Mador Gilmore, "The Saloon as a Club," *The North American Review* 157 (1893): 511-512.

industry. The cocktail suffered as a result, all too often becoming an overly sweet, indifferent concoction to be ridiculed as kitsch and drunk by artifacts.

This is the cocktail's recent history. But thankfully it is not its current status, nor its future. Thanks to some dedicated professionals across the country (and in a few other countries as well), the cocktail has resumed its rightful place at the bar. And, when I see the pride with which Katie Stipe serves up Jerri Banks' superb Juniperitivo at the Flatiron Lounge on Nineteenth Street in Manhattan, I stop worrying about whether or not the cocktail will survive. It is alive and well.

Let's all celebrate this year, which is thankfully not an election year. Let's on the 200th anniversary of the word "cocktail," take pause to remember the fine folks who fought for campaign reform, first-amendment rights, democracy and equality and, most of all, those cocktail heroes who professionalized the industry and refined the art of mixology from the realm of bittered slings and transformed the cocktail into the icon it is today.

Our Heritage in the Mint Julep

BY LENELL SMOTHERS

A regional specialty in the annals of American libational cuisine, the Mint Julep is a venerable predecessor to the cocktail. In the US, this early eye-opener began as a rum-based drink consumed by colonial farmers and progressed into a grand vehicle for the presentation of a true American spirit—bourbon. LeNell Smothers takes us through the fascinating history of the drink, its ingredients, its rituals, and its recipes.

They say that you may always know the grave of
a Virginian as, from the quantity of julep he has drunk,
mint invariably springs up where he has been buried."

—FREDERICK MARRYAT, 1839[37]

THE HISTORY

WHAT CAN BE MORE REFRESHING on a hot, humid summer day than burying your nose in sprigs of mint hanging over the edge of a frosty silver julep cup? Richard Barksdale Harwell was so inspired by this drink that he wrote a book on its history called *The Mint Julep* saying, "Wherever there is a Mint Julep, there is a bit of the Old South...It is nectar to the Virginian, mother's milk to the Kentuckian, and ambrosia to Southerners anywhere."[38]

The history of this drink traces back to the French word *julep*. The word "julep" comes from the Arabic word *julab*, which is related to the Persian word *gulab*: *Gul* means "rose" and *ab* means "water."[39] Those wonderful doughnut-like balls soaked in sweetened, rose scented syrup called *gulab jamun* at an Indian restaurant may come to mind. European crusaders brought the word "*julab*" home from the Arabs sometime in the medieval period.[40] The word evolved into "julep" to refer to sweetened syrups.

---

37. Richard Barksdale Harwell, *The Mint Julep* (Charlottesville, VA: University of Virginia Press, 1985), 17.

38. Ibid.

39. http://www.foodreference.com/html/artmintjulep.html (accessed December 1, 2005).

40. Gary Regan, "Derby is done, but summer is the perfect time for Mint Juleps," *Nation's Restaurant News*, May 24, 1999; sourced through www.findarticles.com/p/articles/mi_m3190/is_21_33/ai_54765133#continue (accessed January 13, 2006).

As is the case with the history of many drinks, sweet-ened syrups often served as a more pleasant way to deliver medicine. Dictionary definitions of the word "julep" refer to medicinal uses. The 1913 *Webster's Revised Unabridged Dictionary* defines it as a "refreshing drink flavored with aromatic herbs; esp. (Med.), a sweet, demulcent, acidulous, or mucilaginous mixture, used as a vehicle." A second definition in this edition elaborates on the modern refer-ence as a "beverage composed of brandy, whisky, or some other spirituous liquor, with sugar, pounded ice, and sprigs of mint;—called also Mint Julep. [U.S.][41]

Although sweetened syrups served medicinal purposes, these syrups were also drunk for pleasure. John Milton writes of such a pleasurable concoction as early as 1634 in *Comus*:

Why are you vexed, Lady? why do you frown?
Here dwell no frowns, nor anger; from these gates
Sorrow flies far.
See here be all the pleasures
That fancy can beget on youthfull thoughts,
When the fresh blood grows lively, and returns
Brisk as the April buds in Primrose-season.
And first behold this cordial Julep here
That flames, and dances in his crystal bounds
With spirits of balm, and fragrant Syrops mixt,
Not that Nepenthes which the wife of Thone,
In Egypt gave to Jove-born Helena
Is of such power to stir up joy as this
To life so friendly, or so cool to thirst.[42]

---

41. http://www.dictionary.net/julep (accessed October 5, 2006).
42. John Milton, *Comus*, see http://whitewolf.newcastle.edu.au/words/authors/M/MiltonJohn/verse/p1/comus.html (accessed February 2, 2006).

The American Museum, one of the first successful magazines in early America, debuted in 1797 in Philadelphia. This publication reports on page fifteen of the first volume that the typical Virginian got out of bed at 6:00 A.M. and drank a "julep made of rum, water, and sugar, but very strong."[43] An English traveler named Captain Frederick Marryat of the British Royal Navy was a celebrated fiction writer in the early nineteenth century who captured this ceremony of American life in his diary writings during his trips through America.[44] Early American settlers drank juleps for breakfast like coffee is drunk today. Chris Morris, master distiller of Woodford Reserve bourbon, says "One sip and Pow! The farmers were ready to face the long day."[45]

Harwell claims that the earliest description of the Mint Julep after it became a common drink in bars and taverns is found in the writings of Charles Joseph Latrobe. Latrobe reported on the meetings of the Anti-Temperance Society in Tallahassee, Florida around 1836. He asks:

> And pray, what is mint julep? I hear you ask. I've got the receipt in my notebook,—let me see—under the head "democratic drinks."—"Take your mint, fresh and unbruised, and put it in a clean tumbler; pour—"but no! I would rather not tell you, for who knows, if once you get the recipe you may be tempted to set to and make the liquor...Who knows, that if you get hold of the recipe, instead of being an orderly, sober member of society, a loyal subject, and a good Tory; you will get muzzy, and hot-brained, and begin to fret about reform, and democratic forms of government,—doubt your Bible—despise your country—hate your King—fight cocks, and race like a Virginian.[46]

---

43. Richard Barksdale Harwell, *The Mint Julep* (Charlottesville, VA: University of Virginia Press, 1985), 6.

44. Ibid, 14-19.

45. "History of Mint Julep," http://www.cocktailtimes.com/history/history_mintjulep.shtml (accessed November 12, 2005).

46. Richard Barksdale Harwell, *The Mint Julep* (Charlottesville, VA: University of Virginia Press, 1985), 12-13.

Harwell also refers to Captain Marryat's description of a Fourth of July celebration in New York City in 1837. Marryat wrote, "…the booths were loaded with porter, ale, cider, mead, brandy, wine, ginger-beer, pop, soda-water, whiskey, rum, punch, gin slings, cocktails, Mint Juleps, besides many other compounds…".[47] Harwell goes on to include Marryat's description of an American hotel bar to be "generally a very large room on the basement, fitted up very much like our gin palaces in London, not so elegant in its decorations indeed, but on the same system. A long counter runs across it, behind which stand two or three barkeepers to wait upon the customers, and distribute the various potations, compounded from several rows of bottles behind them. Here the eye reposes on masses of pure crystal ice, large bunches of mint, decanters of every sort of wine, every variety of spirits, lemons, sugar, bitters…"[48] Clearly, mint was no foreigner to the bar.

THE MINT

Mint has inspired love and turmoil, making a good story even in mythology. Menthe was a nymph loved by Pluto. Proserpine was obviously not too happy with this affection and turned Menthe into a plant.[49]

No one has been able to pinpoint when the addition of mint in a julep first occurred. Mint is not mentioned in a reference to the julep until 1803 in John Davis' *Travels of Four Years and a Half in the United States of America: During 1798, 1799, 1800, 1801, and 1802*. In his writings, Davis

---

47. Ibid, 14.
48. Ibid, 16.
49. M. Grieve, "Spearmint," *A Modern Herbal* http://botanical.com/botanical/mgmh/m/mints-39.html#spe (accessed October 29, 2005).

confirms the morning julep routine by defining a julep as "a dram of spirituous liquor that has mint in it, taken by Virginians of a morning."[50] Captain Marryat penned his observations of American drinking habits in A Diary in America and mentions mint as an ingredient as early as Volume I, Chapter 17 where he writes, "in the evening we looked at the moon, spouted verses, and drank Mint Juleps.[51]

No one knows the exact origin of the Mint Julep, but one legend is that a nineteenth century Kentucky boatman on the Mississippi River went ashore in search of spring water to mix with his bourbon. The mint aroma enticed him to add some to his drink.[52] One can often find mint growing along American spring banks so it is no wonder that mint replaced rose petals in early American juleps.

Peppermint is the mint most often found in moist, spring bank environs.[53] However, spearmint, or common English garden mint, menthe spicata, is the mint of choice in a julep, according to Colonel Joe Nickel, author of The Kentucky Mint Julep.[54] This mint can easily be found in many states in the US, and is believed to have been introduced to the US by settlers from Europe. The English received it from the Romans where it was widely used. Philosopher Pliny the Elder says of it: "The smell of Mint does stir up the minde and the taste to a greedy desire of meate."[55]

50. Richard Barksdale Harwell, The Mint Julep (Charlottesville, VA: University of Virginia Press, 1985), 6.

51. Captain Frederick Marryat, Diary in America, http://www.athelstane.co.uk/marryat/diaramer/diarx/diarx17.htm (accessed January 30, 2006).

52. "The Mint Julep: You Don't Have to Be at the Kentucky Derby to Enjoy One," http://www.thatsthespirit.com/en/drinks/articles/Mint_Julep.asp

53. M. Grieve, "Peppermint," A Modern Herbal, http://botanical.com/botanical/mgmh/m/mints-39.html#pep (accessed October 29, 2005).

54. Colonel Joe Nickell, The Kentucky Mint Julep (Lexington, KY: University Press of Kentucky, 2003), 7.

55. M. Grieve, "Peppermint," A Modern Herbal, http://botanical.com/botanical/mgmh/m/mints-39.html#pep (accessed October 29, 2005).

Supposedly mint was planted at Churchill Downs in Louisville so that Mint Juleps could be served at the very first Kentucky Derby in 1875. Over 6,000 dozen bunches of mint are delivered to Churchill Downs and local groceries the week of the Derby.[56] The mint delivered to Churchill Downs is used for garnish only.

Spearmint may be the preferred type for many people, but juleps can be made from any mint. Other mints worth exploring include chocolate (*Mentha piperita*), pineapple (*Mentha suaveolens 'Variegata'*), apple (*Mentha suaveolens Ehrh*), orange (*Mentha x piperita x citrate*), and lime (*Mentha x piperita f. citrate*). Some of these mints arrived from Europe and others are hybrid crosses.

THE LIQUOR

Social historian Gerald Carson writes in *The Social History of Bourbon*, "Of all the compatibles man has discovered in the world of food and drink, none excels in harmony with which mint blends into a silver goblet filled with ice, a dusting of sugar and several ounces of mellow bourbon."[57] However, the first Mint Juleps were made with rum, brandy, or rye whiskey in the 1700s. Recipes for juleps made from various liquors are recorded in cocktail books even in the early 1900s.

Tom Bullock includes a recipe for an "Overall Julep—St. Louis Style" in his 1917 publication, *The Ideal Bartender*,

---

56. Chuck Martin, "Myth of the Mint Julep," The Cincinnati Enquirer on the Web, April 30, 2003, http://www.enquirer.com/editions/2003/04/30/tem_food30lede.html (accessed May 20, 2005).

57. Gerald Carson, *The Social History of Bourbon: An Unhurried Account of Our Star-Spangled American Drink* (New York: Dodd, Mead, 1963), 214.

where whiskey and gin are mentioned.[58] In *The Savoy Cocktail Book*, Harry Craddock refers to Captain Marryat's recipe that uses mint sprigs, sugar, peach and common brandy, pounded ice, and fresh pineapple. Craddock also includes a recipe for a "Pineapple Julep" that includes maraschino, gin, and sweet white wine.[59]

Around 1845, Harwell claims that a wealthy South Carolinian farmer named William Heyward Trappier visited New College, Oxford in England and was astonished no one knew how to make a Mint Julep. He left an endowment to provide it, and his memory is still honored every June 1st with Mint Juleps served on this date. His julep is reminiscent of Marryat's with a base of apricot brandy with bourbon as the "secret ingredient."[60]

In a letter printed in Jerry Thomas' 1862 book *How to Mix Drinks or The Bon-Vivant's Companion* Captain Marryat wrote that the ingredients in a "real" Mint Julep were peach brandy and common brandy and that "epicures rub the lips of the tumbler with a piece of fresh pineapple."[61] Captain Marryat found juleps "like the American ladies, irresistible."[62] Thomas includes recipes for a brandy julep, a gin julep, and a pineapple julep in addition to a whiskey julep. Harwell writes, in his book *The Mint Julep*, "The listing of the whiskey julep is important as the first recorded bartender's recipe of what has come to be the twentieth-century Mint Julep, though ingenious Kentuckians and

58. Tom Bullock, *The Ideal Bartender* (St. Louis: Buxton & Skinner printing and stationery co., c1917), 43.

59. Harry Craddock, *The Savoy Cocktail Book* (New York: Smith, 1930), 207.

60. Richard Barksdale Harwell, *The Mint Julep* (Charlottesville, VA: University of Virginia Press, 1985), 23.

61. Gary Regan, "Derby is done, but summer is the perfect time for Mint Juleps," *Nation's Restaurant News*, May 24, 1999; sourced through www.findarticles.com/p/articles/mi_m3190/is_21_33/ai_54765133#continue (accessed January 13, 2006).

62. Harry Craddock, *The Savoy Cocktail Book* (New York: Smith, 1930), 207.

Virginians thought out this version for themselves long before."[63]

Early American whiskey was nothing like what we drink today. Whiskey was part of everyday life with farmer's making liquor for easier storage and transport of their grain. Whiskey was used as currency even. The grain liquor was drunk raw without oak aging in the way that we are accustomed to today. Perhaps this rougher whiskey was made more palatable by adding flavorings to make juleps. No one can pinpoint an exact date when bourbon became more common than other liquors in julep making.

The first reference to a darker whiskey probably closer to bourbon as we know it today comes from a letter written in 1849. Another reference to red liquor exists in Herman Melville's 1851 novel *Moby Dick*.[64] Although bourbon whiskey was making a name for itself in places like New Orleans in the late 1700s, this new "red" whiskey aged in charred oak barrels was not widely available until later on in the nineteenth century.

American distillers made whiskey from rye long before the corn-based bourbon whiskey became popular so early juleps surely included rye. Rye whiskey production, however, never recovered after Prohibition, as corn was cheaper and easier to work with. Distillers found corn based whiskey an easier way to jumpstart whiskey production and refill the coffers after the repeal in 1933. Bourbon became America's native spirit, declared so by an Act of Congress in 1964. Rye whiskey has never caught up in favor and is forgotten in modern Mint Julep recipes.

---

63. Richard Barksdale Harwell, *The Mint Julep* (Charlottesville, VA: University of Virginia Press, 1985), 21.

64. Chuck K. Cowdery, *Bourbon Straight: The Uncut and Unfiltered Story of American Whiskey* (Chicago: Made and Bottled in Kentucky, 2004), 33.

Here are a few tips on using bourbon in juleps. Using a rich, robust bourbon with a proof of at least 86 to 90 holds up better than an 80 proof version since so much ice is added. A bottled in bond label guarantees at least 100 proof with power to hold up even better with the dilution. A spicy bourbon with a nice rye component in the mashbill such as Wild Turkey, Bulleit, or Old Grand Dad, will hold up to more sugar in the julep. If you use a gentler, sweeter bourbon, use less sugar. Wheated bourbons such as Maker's Mark, Van Winkle, Rebel Yell, Weller, and Old Fitzgerald fall into the gentler, sweeter category.

Generally, the better the bourbon the better the julep. However, Julian Van Winkle, owner of the Rip Van Winkle label, which signifies a mighty fine bourbon, says "I don't drink 'em unless I have to. I'd rather just drink my whiskey without all that crap in there."[65] The Van Winkle family surely made some fine juleps at Derby Day parties held during the prime years of their leadership at the now defunct Stitzel-Weller Distillery. Some bourbons, like the few remaining rare bottles of the Very Very Old Fitzgerald from Stitzel-Weller, are now too sacred for juleps. The better the bourbon the better the julep, but some bourbons are just too good, and all bourbon is good enough.

THE CUPS

Metal drinking cups without handles existed long before the Mint Julep, although now the Mint Julep cup is the moniker for this design. Metal cups are sturdy and travel easily. This style of cup became connected with agriculture and racing in the early part of the nineteenth

---

65. Interview with Julian Van Winkle on August 26, 2004.

century when cups were awarded as prizes at fairs and races according to Pat Burnett of Wakefield-Scearce Galleries in Shelbyville, Kentucky.[66] A specially designed julep cup is presented to the Kentucky Derby winner each year.[67] Brown-Waterhouse-Kaiser acts as the exclusive source for the Official Kentucky Derby Mint Julep Cup.[68] Salisbury Pewter researched drinking cups dating all the way back to the 1700s and now offers reproduction cups representing the different craftsman from states like Alabama, New York, and, of course Kentucky.[69]

In 1816, the Kentucky Gazette talks about Mint Julep cups being given at horse races in the Commonwealth.[70] According to the Derby Museum, the Mint Julep became Churchill Downs' signature drink in 1938 when they started to serve the drink in souvenir glasses for 75 cents a drink.[71] For the last twenty years, however, Churchill Downs has served juleps from a bottled mix, called "Early Times Mint Julep Cocktail," with more than 140,000 cups made every Kentucky Derby week.[72] With this type of bottled concoction removing part of the ceremony and romance, it is no wonder few people today have had a Mint Julep outside of Derby events.

The Derby Museum has a complete collection of commemorative official Mint Julep glasses. Each year the

66. Julie Cole, "Mint Julep Cups," *Southern Accents on the Web*, http://www.southernaccents.com/accents/print/0,15217,445547,00.html (accessed February 2, 2006).

67. "Brown-Waterhouse-Kaiser Jewelers Presents the Official Kentucky Mint Julep Cup," http://kyjulep.com/ (accessed February 2, 2006).

68. Brown-Waterhouse-Kaiser Jewelers "Homepage," http://brownwaterhousejewelers.com/ (accessed February 2, 2006).

69. "The Historic Cup Collection on the Web," http://www.salisburypewter.com/salsite/pdf/salpdf6.pdf (accessed February 3, 2006).

70. Chuck Martin, "Myth of the Mint Julep," *The Cincinnati Enquirer on the Web*, April 30, 2003, http://www.enquirer.com/editions/2003/04/30/tem_food30lede.html (accessed May 20, 2005).

71. "The Mint Julep," http://www.kentuckyderby.com/2006/derby_experience/mint_julep.html (accessed January 3, 2006).

72. "The Mint Julep," http://www.earlytimes.com/derby/mint_julep.asp (accessed January 3, 2006).

Derby glass has a different design usually combining horses and the Downs. The first souvenir glass was made in 1938 with a simple horse and horseshoe design. In 1945 the first souvenir Mint Julep glasses by Libbey Glass Company were made for Harry M. Stevens Inc., the concessionaire at Churchill Downs. There were two sizes, a tall one for the Zombie and a short one for the Mint Julep. A shot glass was also made. Due to post war shortages, there were no glasses made in 1946 and 1947.[73]

The price of silver makes this a luxury item for Mint Julep cocktails. Pewter is less expensive and works just as well to develop the nice frost on the glass that helps maintain the chill of the drink. Aluminum is the least expensive metal for cups and also works well. Glass is the least preferred type of cup as it warms much more easily, but you can make a fine julep in a well-chilled highball glass as a last resort, with many mixologists preferring a Collins glass, when metal is not available.

THE RECIPES

Like the martini, different preferences abound for the Mint Julep. There are the muddlers and the non-muddlers. Some folks use mint for flavor while others only use it for bouquet. Some folks add simple syrup or powdered sugar while others prefer whiskey poured right over the ice with no sweeteners. Early twentieth-century newspaperman Irvin S. Cobb believed that "a man who would let the crushed leaves and the mangled stemlets steep in the finished decoction would put scorpions in a baby's bed."[74] Such heated opinions over how to make a proper Mint Julep

---

73. "Art of Spirit: Mint Julep Art," http://cocktailtimes.com/indepth/art/derby_art.shtml (accessed November 11, 2005).

have existed for years as humorously told in the 1936 copy of *Cobb's Own Recipe Book*, "...well, down our way we've always had a theory that the Civil War was not brought on by Secession or Slavery or the State's Rights issue. These matters contributed to the quarrel, but there is a deeper reason. It was brought on by some Yankee coming down south and putting nutmeg in a julep. So our folks just up and left the Union flat."[75] His recipe follows:

> Put 12 sprigs of fresh mint in bowl, covered with powdered sugar and just enough water to dissolve the sugar, and crush with wooden pestle. Place half the crushed mint and liquid in the bottom of a crackled glass tumbler, or in sterling silver or pewter tankard. Fill glass half full of finely crushed ice. Add rest of crushed mint and fill remainder of glass with crushed ice. Pour in whisky until glass is brimming. Place in ice-box a least an hour (preferably two or three hours—if you can wait that long). Decorate with sprigs of mint covered with powdered sugar when ready to serve.[76]

One story relates how Kentucky Senator Henry Clay introduced the Mint Julep to Washington in the early 1800s. The historic landmark hotel now known as the Willard InterContinental, located on Pennsylvania Avenue in DC, is where Senator Clay shared his Kentucky heritage with Captain Marryat in the form of this recipe, which surely involved an argument over how to make a proper julep:

> The mint leaves fresh and tender, should be pressed against the goblet with the back of a silver spoon. Only bruise the leaves gently and then remove them from the goblet. Half fill with cracked ice. Mellow bourbon, aged in oaken barrels, is poured from the jigger and allowed to slide slowly

---

74. "Miscellaneous: Mint Juleps," November 14, 2005, http://wiki.wbar.org/index.php/Miscellaneous (accessed February 28, 2006).

75. Colonel Joe Nickell, *The Kentucky Mint Julep* (Lexington, KY: University Press of Kentucky, 2003), 21.

76. Ibid, 34.

through the cracked ice. In another receptacle, granulated sugar is slowly mixed with chilled limestone water to make a silvery mixture as smooth as some rare Egyptian oil, then poured on top of the ice. While beads of moisture gather on the burnished exterior of the silver goblet, garnish the brim of the goblet with choicest sprigs of mint.[77]

Although Jerry Thomas did not create the Mint Julep recipe, his recording of it in his 1862 *The Bon-Vivant* provided guidance for bartenders. His Mint Julep is brandy based with the whiskey julep a variation thereof:

WHISKEY JULEP.
(Use large bar-glass.)
The whiskey julep is made the same
as the mint julep, omitting all fruits and berries.

MINT JULEP.
(Use large bar-glass.)
Take one table-spoonful of white pulverized sugar.
one-half table-spoonfuls of water, mix well with a spoon.
one and one-half wine-glass full of brandy.
Take three or four sprigs of fresh mint, and press them well in the sugar and water, until the flavor of the mint is extracted ; add the brandy, and fill the glass with finely shaved ice, then draw out the sprigs of mint and insert them in the ice with the stems downward, so that the leaves will be above, in the shape of a bouquet; arrange berries, and small pieces of sliced orange on top in a tasty manner, dash with Jamaica rum, and serve with a straw.[78]

Tom Bullock outlines a "Mint Julep—Kentucky Style" in his book *The Ideal Bartender:*

77. "Editorial Review," http://www.washingtonpost.com/ac2/wp-dyn/?node=cityguide/profile&id=1079311 (accessed February 20, 2006).
78. Jerry Thomas, *Bar-Tenders Guide, or How to Mix Drinks*, 1862, sourced through http://www.theartofdrink.com/book/pg16.php (accessed February 27, 2006).

MINT JULEP—KENTUCKY STYLE

Use a large Silver Mug.
Dissolve one lump of Sugar in one-half pony of Water.
Fill mug with Fine Ice.
Two jiggers of Old Bourbon Whiskey.
Stir well; add one boquet (sp.) of Mint and serve.
Be careful and not bruise the Mint.[79]

Perhaps Gary Regan would have loved to have a sip at Bullock's bar. Similar to Bullock's recipe, he instructs that the mint is just for aromatic garnish in the *Bartender's Bible*.[80] However, Regan goes on to include a recipe for a muddled julep in his Bible and also supports the minted simple syrup in *The Joy of Mixology*.[81]

Colonel Joe Nickel, author of *The Kentucky Mint Julep*, disagrees with this notion of the mint only for bouquet, writing that it "defies tradition and logic."[82] He offers this version:

5 sprigs of fresh mint
1 teaspoon granulated sugar
2-3 teaspoons hot water
crushed ice
2 ounces. bourbon

In a measuring cup, place 4 mint sprigs and sugar and add hot water. Stir. Allow to steep and cool. Meanwhile, fill a julep cup with crushed ice, add bourbon, and stir. Returning to the mint, use a spoon to press the leaves against the side of the cup, then remove. Pour the syrup over the bourbon and again stir until cup is frosted. Garnish with remaining mint sprig.[83]

---

79. Tom Bullock, *The Ideal Bartender* (St. Louis: Buxton & Skinner printing and stationery co., c1917), 43.

80. Gary Regan, *The Bartender's Bible* (Harper Collins: New York, 1991), 29.

81. Gary Regan, *The Joy of Mixology* (Clarkson Potter: New York, 2003), 303.

82. Colonel Joe Nickell, *The Kentucky Mint Julep* (Lexington, KY: University Press of Kentucky, 2003), 8.

83. Ibid, 43.

General Simon Bolivar Buckner (killed on Okinawa June 18, 1945) laid out directions for a twentieth-century julep in a quite poetic letter to a fellow general:

March 30, 1937

My Dear General Connor:

Your letter requesting my formula for mixing mint juleps leaves me in the same position in which Captain Barber found himself when asked how he was able to carve the image of an elephant from a block of wood. He said that it was a simple process consisting merely of whittling off the part that didn't look like an elephant.

The preparation of the quintessence of gentlemanly beverages can be described only in like terms. A mint julep is not a product of a formula. It is a ceremony and must be performed by a gentleman possessing a true sense of the artistic, a deep reverence for the ingredients and a proper appreciation of the occasion. It is a rite that must not be entrusted to a novice, a statistician nor a Yankee. It is a heritage of the Old South, and emblem of hospitality, and a vehicle in which noble minds can travel together upon the flower-strewn paths of a happy and congenial thought.

So far as the mere mechanics of the operation are concerned, the procedure, stripped of its ceremonial embellishments, can be described as follows:

Go to a spring where cool, crystal-clear water bubbles from under a bank of dew-washed ferns. In a consecrated vessel, dip up a little water at the source. Follow the stream thru its banks of green moss and wild flowers until it broadens and trickles thru beds of mint growing in aromatic profusion and waving softly in the summer breeze. Gather the sweetest and tenderest shoots and gently carry them home. Go to the sideboard and select a decanter of Kentucky Bourbon distilled by a master hand, mellowed with age, yet still vigorous and inspiring. An ancestral sugar bowl, a row of silver goblets, some spoons and some ice and you are ready to start.

Into a canvas bag pound twice as much ice as you think you will need. Make it fine as snow, keep it dry and do not allow it to degenerate into slush. Into each goblet, put a slightly heaping teaspoonful of granulated sugar, barely cover this with spring water and slightly bruise one mint leaf into this, leaving the spoon in the goblet. Then pour elixir from the decanter until the goblets are about one-fourth full. Fill the goblets with snowy ice, sprinkling in a small amount of sugar as you fill. Wipe the outside of the goblets dry, and embellish copiously with mint.

Then comes the delicate and important operation of frosting. By proper manipulation of the spoon, the ingredients are circulated and blended until nature, wishing to take a further hand and add another of its beautiful phenomena, encrusts the whole in a glistening coat of white frost.

Thus harmoniously blended by the deft touches of a skilled hand, you have a beverage eminently appropriate for honorable men and beautiful women.

When all is ready, assemble your guests on the porch or in the garden where the aroma of the juleps will rise heavenward and make the birds sing. Propose a worthy toast, raise the goblets to your lips, bury your nose in the mint, inhale a deep breath of its fragrance and sip the nectar of the gods.

Being overcome with thirst, I can write no further.
Sincerely,
Lt. Gen. S.B. Buckner, Jr.
VMI Class of 1906[84]

Even Master Distillers will give you different opinions on how to make a perfect Mint Julep. The president of Maker's Mark, Bill Samuels, Jr., writes in his autobiography, "The Mint Julep may very well be the finest mixed drink in the world. But hardly anyone has tasted a good one, so it is viewed by most as a pretty unfortunate taste experience." He refers to three common mistakes people

---

84. "The Mint Julep," October 1, 2002, http://www.civilwarhome.com/mintjulep. htm (accessed February 2, 2006).

make with their juleps: 1) using an overbearing bourbon, 2) using too much mint, and 3) using too much sugar. Mr. Samuels prefers infusing mint into his bourbon for juleps.[85] The following recipe from his book is best for a crowd, because you can make the basic mixture several days ahead, then add ice.

I bottle of Maker's Mark
Lots of fresh spearmint
Distilled water
Granulated sugar
Powdered sugar

1. To prepare the mint extract, remove about 40 small mint leaves—wash and place in small mixing bowl. Cover with 3 ounces of Maker's Mark. Allow the leaves to soak for 15 minutes. Then gather the leaves in a clean, soap-free peace of cotton cloth and vigorously wring the mint bundle over the bowl of whiskey. Dip the bundle again and repeat the process several times. Then set aside.

2. To prepare the simple syrup, mix a cup of granulated sugar and a cup of water in a cooking pot. Heat to dissolve the sugar. Stir constantly so the sugar does not burn. Set aside to cool.

3. To prepare the julep mixture, pour 3 1/2 cups of Maker's Mark into a large glass bowl or glass pitcher. (Pour the remaining whiskey from the liter bottle into another container and save it for another purpose.) Add 1 cup of the simple syrup to the Maker's Mark.

4. Now, begin adding the mint extract 1 tablespoon at a time to the julep mixture. Each batch of mint extract is different, so you must taste and smell after each tablespoon is added. You may have to leave the room a time or two to cleanse your nose. The tendency is to use too much mint. You are looking for a soft mint aroma and taste—generally about 3 tablespoons.

5. When you think it's right, pour the whole mixture back

---

85. Bill Samuels, Jr., *My Autobiography* (Louisville, KY: Saber Publishing, 2000),

into the empty liter bottle and refrigerate it for at least 24 hours to "marry" the flavors.

6. To serve the mint julep, fill each glass (preferably a silver julep cup) half full with shaved ice. Insert a sprig of mint, then pack in more ice to about an inch over the top of the cup. Then, insert a straw that has been cut to one inch above the top of the cup so the nose is forced close to the mint when sipping the julep.

7. When frost forms on the cup, pour the refrigerated julep mixture over the ice and add a sprinkle of powdered sugar to the top of the ice. Then prop your feet up and enjoy.[86]

This julep recipe, from Master Distiller Chris Morris, is for a "mint muddler":

3-5 mint leaves
I teaspoon powdered sugar
2 teaspoon water
2-2.5 ounces Woodford Reserve Bourbon
Crushed Ice

Muddle (stir/gentle crush) four mint springs and sugar in the bottom of a julep glass. Add water and continue to muddle. Add Woodford Reserve Bourbon. Pack the julep glass with crushed ice. Add a mint sprig for decoration and sipping straw. If a metal julep cup is used, be sure to use a wooden muddler (bottom of a wooden spoon) instead of metal spoon. This will eliminate the possibility of any metal shavings getting into the drink or scratching the julep cup.[87]

When fed up with all the complications of juleps, there's the recipe attributed to Henry Watterson, a famed Kentucky newspaper man from days of old. He insisted that two glasses be used. Pour the bourbon into the first glass. The other glass holds the mint, sugar, and water. He urges to throw that mixture out and just drink the whiskey.[88]

---

86. Ibid, 69.

87. "Mint Julep Recipe from Woodford Reserve Master Distiller Chris Forman," http://www.brown-forman.com/products/Recipe%20Archive/2005%20Derby%20Recipes.htm (accessed February 27, 2006).

88. Colonel Joe Nickell, *The Kentucky Mint Julep* (Lexington, KY: University Press of Kentucky, 2003), 20.

Experiment using some of these basics:

- Frost glass or preferably a metal mug well before serving. Placing cups in the freezer for about half an hour will suffice. A well-chilled cup helps prevent the ice from melting so quickly. Avoid touching the sides once the cup is frosted to prevent unsightly smudges.

- No matter what type you use, always use the freshest mint, whether infusing the mint into the whiskey or sugar syrup, muddling it in the bottom of the glass, or just using as a garnish. Tender young leaves are the best. Keep mint sprigs in a glass of water in the refrigerator if not used immediately upon harvesting or purchasing. When infusing or muddling, strip the mint leaves and discard the tough stems, which can add bitterness.

- Use good bourbon. Some might argue that there is no "bad" bourbon.

- Use shaved or finely crushed ice. You can make your own at home by wrapping ice cubes in a clean dishtowel and crushing it with a rolling pin or frying pan. A snow cone machine makes quick shaved ice, especially if making many drinks where shaving ice by hand becomes cumbersome.

- Position the mint garnish and straw carefully. Mint juleps may be the only cocktail that relies on its garnish to enhance the olfactory experience. Shove the straw through the ice all the way to the bottom of the cup, and then cut it off just above the top of the ice. Position the sprig of mint near the straw so that you can inhale the scent of the mint while sipping.

Drink Mint Juleps when it is hot to cool you off, when the weather is cold to warm you up, when you are sad to perk you up, when you are happy to celebrate life. Drink mint juleps.

As in the famous words of Lt. Gen. S.B. Buckner, Jr,, "Being overcome with thirst, I can write no further."[89]

---

89. "The Mint Julep" October 1, 2002, http://www.civilwarhome.com/mintjulep. htm (accessed February 2, 2006).

The BIRTH
OF THE PINKS

BEING THE WHOLE AND TRUE STORY, OR STORIES,
BEHIND THE CREATION OF THE LAST TRUE
CLASSIC COCKTAIL TO BE BORN IN THE
TWENTIETH CENTURY

BY GARY REGAN

*It's pink. It's classic. It's been claimed
to be created by more than one well-known
mixologist. And now Gary Regan reports
to us the origins of the modern classic that
took the United States by storm thanks
to the HBO cable television series*
Sex and the City.

COINTREAU MADE HER UP. That was our conclusion when, after years of trying to track down the mysterious Cheryl Cook, supposed creator of the Cosmopolitan cocktail, Mardee and I came up empty handed. I believe it was William Grimes, of *The New York Times*, who first mentioned Cook's name to us, and the good folk at Cointreau agreed. "She's somewhere in Miami," they told us. This all took place in the mid-1990s, when e-mail was, to us at least, in its infancy, so all of our tracking had to be done via phone, and by snail mail. How very tedious.

Cointreau was probably the chief beneficiary of the Cosmo explosion, although many versions were made with generic triple sec. Those in the know, however, usually went the Cointreau route, loving the liqueur for it's dry sophistication, as well as its intense orange zest flavors. And Absolut Citron probably fared well too because of this, now classic, cocktail, but many other citrus-flavored vodkas appeared on the heels of the Absolut bottling, so it probably had to share the jackpot with the rest of the products that threw their figurative hats into the ring.

It seemed to make sense to us, though, that the marketing department at Cointreau created the drink, and someone there invented a fictitious bartender who they touted as having created the drink. That would add legitimacy to the cocktail, right? We thought that Cointreau was behind this for many a year.

Various other people were credited with having invented the Cosmo along the way, though the two people who were cited most often both vigorously denied that they were the ones to first mix the pink drink. Dale DeGroff, King Cocktail himself, claimed that he first sampled Cosmopolitans at the Fog City Diner in San Francisco, and again at New York's Odeon, and in both cases they were made with Absolut Citron, Rose's Lime Juice, and cranberry juice. Dale simply added Cointreau to the mix, and used fresh lime juice instead of Rose's, when he introduced the drink to his customers at the Rainbow Room in 1996.

Toby Cecchini, in his book, *Cosmopolitan: A Bartender's Life* (New York: Broadway 2003), says that he first encountered Cosmos at the Odeon when they were introduced to him, circa 1987, by his co-worker, Melissa Huffsmith, aka Mesa. Mesa had worked at the Life Café in San Francisco, and the drink that she knew as the Cosmopolitan, as served at Life, was made with plain old vodka, Rose's, and grenadine. Uuurgh. Cecchini didn't much care for the drink, but he did sort of go for the pink, so he re-invented it using Citron vodka, Cointreau, fresh lime juice, and cranberry juice.

When I read about this in Cecchini's book, I thought to myself, Goddammit, man, you did, too, invent the Cosmopolitan. Why so shy? And I wrote as much for *Cheers* magazine in 2005 when they asked me to pen a piece about the origins of various drinks. Although I'd met him only once, in early 2004, I had a soft spot for Toby. I should fill you in.

In September 2004, Mardee and I published a review of Cecchini's book in our e-mail newsletter, *Ardent Spirits*. Here's an excerpt from the review:

> Cecchini's denial of responsibility for the Cosmo isn't the only thing that's annoying about this book, but we're still recommending that you run out and buy Cosmopolitan, the book, immediately. Why? Because Cecchini, love him or hate him, has the soul of a true bartender, and it fair shines from the pages of this book.
>
> Toby has an annoying habit of using words that are not only too long for a bartender to know, but also too obscure for most people to understand. He does the same with foreign phrases, too, but once we got over being really tee-

ed off with him for being so obviously over-educated, we got enthralled in his book.

I got hold of Toby's email address, and as soon as we published the newsletter I sent him a link to the review. If you're going to insult someone publicly, I thought, you should be the first person to break it to them. Cecchini replied promptly:

> Gary,
> I just read the review; love it: guilty as charged. If there are two things I want my customers/readers to take away from a brush with me, they are arrogance and annoyance— provided they like whatever else they're imbibing… Thanks for the lovely review.

Now I loved the man.

A few months later I found myself on a press junket to the Cognac region of France with Toby, and various and sundry other scribes, so I posed the question:

"Why do you keep denying having invented the Cosmo?"

"Because nobody ever believed me when I laid claim to the drink," he told me. Fair enough.

It's important, at this part of the story, for you to know the tale of the birth of another drink, the Kamikaze. And it's also important that you understand that this story is strictly as I lived it, not necessarily the truth of the matter.

In the 1970s I was tending bar at Drake's Drum, an earthy joint on Manhattan's Upper East Side. Dave Ridings, an old friend from England who took me in when I arrived on these shores, had gotten me the gig, and it was a job I adored. The same Dave Ridings introduced me to Kamikazes, telling me that Scott Lamb, then a bartender at Botany Bay on East 86th Street, had been the guy who first poured the drink for him. It was made with Stolich-naya vodka, and a few drops of Rose's Lime Juice. Just a few drops, mind you. Stirred over ice, the Kamikaze was strained, normally into a rocks glass, and it was a shooter. A drink to get you drunk. Ridings asked Lamb what the difference was supposed to be between the Kamikaze, and a very dry Vodka Gimlet. "You don't want to commit suicide after a Vodka Gimlet," said Lamb.

Kamikazes ruled on the Upper East Side for many a year. I was there. I witnessed this. Any time there was a lull in the conversation, someone would order up a round of Kamis, and we'd get back on track. Looking for fun in all the wrong places. Kamikazes were magic pills. Guaranteed to get the party going again. And that decade was one, very long, very drunken, and often drug-filled party. It wasn't until years later that I heard about Kamikazes being made with Cointreau and fresh lime juice. Being sipped, instead of gulped. From martini glasses, no less, instead of rocks glasses. How the hell did that happen, I wondered.

But that's how it goes with cocktails. Someone invents a drink. Perhaps two or three or seven people invent the same drink at the same time—this often happens when new products hit the shelves, and cocktailian bartenders don their creative hats to figure out how to use the new bottling. The drink spreads its wings and flies from place to place—or it simply dies on the spot—and every bartender who gets his or her hands on the recipe tweaks it a little. The drink changes. Or it doesn't. Perhaps the name changes. There's just no way to figure out exactly what will happen to any given formula once it makes the round of America's bars. Now let's get back to the Cosmopolitan.

On Sunday, September 25, 2005, at 11:24 P.M. EST, a certain someone in Florida clicked on the "send" button, and transmitted an e-mail to Mardee and me:

Hello Mr. & Mrs. Regan!

I was recently made aware of various articles written about me and the Cosmopolitan. I have also recently purchased your book, 'New Classic Cocktails.'

My name is Cheryl Cook. I was a bartender from 1985-2000 on South Beach. I was commonly refereed to as "The Martini Queen of South Beach." I have spent the past several years working as a Producer & Technical Director in the Event Industry. I also have traveled with a Dance Company around the World for many years. During this period I was out of the "Bar" loop.

The story goes like this.....

A friend, actually the first person I served a Cosmopolitan to, (who also witnessed 15 years of South Beach being "crazy" for Cosmopolitans), found an article a couple of weeks ago giving me credit for the Cosmopolitan and called me.

I served my first Cosmopolitan to Christina Solopuerto the night we received the "First" bottle of Absolut Citron. Christina was sitting at my bar, at The Strand on South Beach" in 1985. The Strand was under the original ownership of, Gary Farmer, Irene Gersing and Mark Benck. Within 30 minutes the entire bar had a Cosmo in front of them. Within 45 minutes the entire restaurant had one. I had already emptied the "one" and only bottle of Absolut Citron, so I had to squeeze lemons into the regular Absolut.

Regarding 'Sex And The City' popularizing this drink; Patricia & Rebecca Fields, the Costume Designers (Mother & Daughter Team) for the entire run of 'Sex And The City' were customers of mine for 15 years. They sat at every bar I ever worked and watched, first hand, the sheer onslaught of South Beach Cosmo drinkers.

By the way, I even named my cat Cosmo!

Any way, thank you for the acknowledgment. I have always kicked myself for not seeing to some kind of recognition.

Thanks for my 15 minutes!

Call or write if you would like.

Cheryl Cook

My God! Cheryl Cook exists. This e-mail made my day.
Now I had to try to verify who she was, and whether or not
she really did invent the Cosmopolitan. Bear in mind that
I don't consider myself to be an investigative reporter. I'm
not even a journalist in my eyes. I'm a writer. I write from
my point of view. And of course, I'm a bartender, too, which
helps me get to the bottom of some cocktail-related stuff,
simply because I know how bartenders' minds work. I fired
a few questions to Cheryl to see how she would respond.
Here's how that went:

1. What was the original recipe?

Absolut Citron a splash of triple sec a drop of roses lime
juice [sic] and just enough cranberry to make it "Oh so pretty
in pink" and topped with a curled lemon twist.

2. How did you come up with the recipe? What made
you put those specific ingredients together?

The Martini had just made it's come back. Women were
ordering them just for the glass but many could not drink them
because they were too strong. My idea was to create a "pretty"
cocktail that they could drink and serve it in a Martini glass.

3. How did you come up with the name?

Cosmopolitan Magazine had done a several page spread on
female Maitre d's and Nathalie Thomas from the Strand was one
of the featured Maitre d's. She had that issue with her daily!

I was sold at this point. This woman obviously created
the drink. But I pressed further. I wanted more evidence.
Here's an excerpt from another e-mail from Cheryl:

I believe it was Southern Wine and Spirits that was handling
the Absolut products at the time . . . I was the Head Bartender
of the Strand on Washington Avenue . . . My Southern Wine
and Spirits rep brought me a new Absolut product, "Absolut
Citron." He said, "create something Cheryl." I love a challenge and I had wanted to create a new drink for the Martini
glass so......The ingredients, as I always phrased it, "Absolut
Citron, a splash of triple sec, a drop of roses lime [sic] and just

enough cranberry to make it oh so pretty in pink," fell in suit. Basically this recipe is a no brainier, mixing wise. Merely a Kamikaze with Absolut Citron and a splash of cranberry juice. My objective was also a "design" task. To create a visually stunning cocktail in a beautiful glass. Pretty and pretty tasty too. Not so much trying to reinvent the wheel, just bringing it up to speed.

For me, this is the sentence that clinched it: Merely a Kamikaze with Absolut Citron and a splash of cranberry juice. That's exactly what the drink is. Cheryl merely took a tried and true recipe and tweaked it a little. She wasn't boasting about her creativity, she was telling it like it was. And Cheryl gives way too many details for this story not to be true. The way in which she came up with the name, for instance, is at once believable. Cheryl Cook is the real deal as far as I'm concerned. God bless her little pink heart!

So the drink made its way across the country, landing in San Francisco, then New York, and along the way, the recipe was butchered. Typical, huh? But just as the drink that I first knew as the Kamikaze, made with only vodka and Rose's, ended up as a cocktail containing Cointreau and fresh lime juice, the bastardized version of Cheryl's original formula fell into the hands of a couple of cocktailian bartenders in the Big Apple who nurtured it, and kissed it back to life. God bless Toby Cecchini's heart, and God bless Dale DeGroff's heart, too.

THE PROFESSION

Before Prohibition, bartenders and mixologists were on a professional plane with psychologists and other professionals—people who provided a service that offered patrons a memorable experience that was perfectly executed time and time again. For a few decades, bartending was considered to be the "job" taken by writers, actors, models, and other celebrity hopefuls to pay the rent rather than a profession that's taken seriously for its own merits. Those times have radically changed. More and more aspirants to the bartending profession are taking the job more seriously, educating themselves by reading classic cocktail books, learning from the seasoned old guard who have been spreading the gospel of the cocktail experience. We asked a few of those cocktail veterans to testify before us in these pages.

During the 1800s, "Professor" Jerry Thomas was famous for his bartending skills and especially the his preparation of a Blue Blazer shown here. (From the collection of Dale DeGroff.)

ENTER
THE MIXOLOGIST

REDISCOVERING THE BAR TENDER'S PASSION

BY ROBERT HESS

More than a liquid, a cocktail is a passionate experience, if executed by an equally passionate professional: a mixologist. Robert Hess, a zealous champion of the bartender's craft, explains why history and a return to the Pre-Prohibition professional standards the industry upheld hold the key to excellence in the future.

COCKTAILS ARE AMERICA'S FIRST internationally recognized cuisine. Today, you can find bartenders not only in San Francisco, Seattle, Toledo, and Rochester, but also in London, Paris, Sydney, Frankfurt, Beijing, Singapore, and Barcelona. It is more than a craft, and more than a trade, it is an art form.

But before there can be art, there must be an artist. And before there can be an artist, there must be passion.

Far too often, bartenders today lack the passion, the spark, and the dedication that is necessary to actually treat the cocktail as a respected craft. More often than not, they are simply working as a bartender until something better comes up, without any perception of it being a true occupation or calling. They might as well be selling newspapers on the corner, or working as a security guard at some abandoned factory.

The common perception of bartending often isn't much different from the stereotype of the position that was rep-resented by Tom Cruise in the movie *Cocktail*. There, the bartender was portrayed as being full of flash and bravado, with bottles flying through the air, and cocktails that were little more than an alcoholic party lubricant. Culinary detail was not even a consideration.

Is this then what the bartender is? Is this what the bartender has always been?

In fact, it is far from it. Sure, a little splash of showman-ship has almost always played a small role in the bartender's craft, but it used to be done with appropriate moderation, and never to the point where it would get in the way of the quality of the drink presented.

If mixed drinks should be called for, it is the bartender's duty to mix and prepare them above the counter, and al-low the customers to see the operation; they should be

prepared in such a neat, quick, and scientific way as to
draw attention.[90]

As seen here, in this quote from an 1888 bartenders' manual, we see that the concept of combining both
exactitude of preparation as well as just enough flair as it
deserved. The drink itself is the object of desire, not its
process of preparation. It is the bartender's culinary abilities
that are in the spotlight, not any flourishes that they might
employ. Any two-bit magician will tell you that the flourishes that they use during their performance are intended
to distract the audience from what they are really doing.
From what I've seen with modern bartenders, those that
rely on theatrics when they prepare a drink, do so because
they similarly need to distract you from thinking too much
about the drink they end up putting before you.

Nobody is born knowing how to bartend. It is a skill
that needs to be learned, or more importantly taught.
Knowledge is thus passed on from master to student, with
some students themselves becoming masters, and capable of
passing on their knowledge on to more and more students.
It is the responsibility of the teacher to really know their
craft and be able to correctly pass that information on to
the students. It is also the responsibility of the student to
not only learn what they are taught, but also to study on
their own in order to continue the education and thus not
only compensate for anything that they might not have
properly paid attention to, but also to achieve knowledge
that their teacher may not have had. This is how human
knowledge expands and grows over time.

History is festooned with incidents where the knowledge of one generation fails to get passed on to the next.
Archeologists are constantly digging up evidence that our

---

90. Harry Johnson, *The New And Improved Illustrated Bartenders' Manual* (New
York: Harry Johnson, 1888), 21.

distant ancestors had technical knowledge that was lost, and would take generations, if not centuries, to be redis-covered. Not far from the art of the bartender, the art of winemaking once suffered such a blow.

Wine, or at least the process of creating fermented beverages out of fruits or grains, has been known since 5400 BC or earlier. Throughout countless generations, this simple task grew into an art form. It was most likely the ancient Greeks who first began evolving the process of making wine into something that was fit for royalty. The Romans expanded upon this knowledge, and as they spread their empire to the distant shores of Europe, they took their grape vines with them. Because they ruled most of Europe for over 600 years of uninterrupted control, they stored within their population countless generations of very intimate knowledge about growing grapes, and producing wines. But that all changed when the Roman Empire fell. It is said that Rome's demise was in part due to being slowly poisoned from lead that lined their wine jugs. Since the art that they had developed was mostly an oral tradition, when the Romans disappeared, so too did all of the centuries of winemaking knowledge that they had amassed. It would take another 600 years before the French monasteries would finally restore the art to its previous Roman glory.

While not nearly the same scope as the fall of the Ro-man Empire, the American cocktail has also suffered from a period of time when the knowledge of its art form was lost and forgotten. This period is known as Prohibition. It lasted from 1920 to 1933, and while not a span of multiple generations, it was long enough to radically influence how the American bartender, and more importantly the American public, would view the cocktail for years to come.

Fortunately, unlike the Roman winemakers, bartending was not just an oral tradition. Many different volumes of

bartender guides exists from the golden age of bartending,
but the amount of missing information can be imagined by
realizing that the cocktail existed since about 1800 (its first
printed definition appeared in 1806), but there would be no
guides that would provide recipes or other guidance until
1862, and little in the way of information that specifically
described the training process and expectations.

During the latter half of the 1800s, the cocktail was
bringing about a very exciting change in the way that people
thought about drinks and drinking. No longer were mixed
drinks simply ways to gussie up the inebriating capabilities
of alcohol, but bartenders were focusing on the potential
of the ingredients being used in order to bring about this
unique American cuisine. Drinks were once simply plugged
into fairly simple categories. Drinks such as the Daisy, Fix,
Flip, Julep, Shrub, Sling, Smash, and Sour were categories
that each represented a fairly straightforward base recipe
which the bartender would simply modify slightly to satisfy
the customer. The Gin Sling, Brandy Sling, Whiskey Sling,
etc., were essentially the same recipe, just using a different
base spirit. The cocktail was originally just yet another
such category, with customers being able to order drinks
with such imaginative names as Champagne Cocktail, Gin
Cocktail, Brandy Cocktail, or when they really wanted to
cut loose, a Fancy Gin Cocktail.

In order for the mixed drink to realize its potential as a
culinary medium, it would be necessary for several separate
accomplishments to come about. The spirituous products
being used needed to be of sufficient quality that there was
no longer any need to disguise their flavors, the general
public would need to be of sufficient means to look towards
alcohol not as a release from their woes, but as a celebration of their accomplishments, and there would need to
be financial means to allow culinary largess. Fortunately,
all of these planets seemed to align about the same time

that Jerry Thomas and his now famous bartender's guide entered the scene.

The cocktail soon became the culinary embodiment of the mixed drink. It represented the first time in which the presented drink was composed of mostly alcoholic ingredients, that didn't need to be disguised by sodas, juices, and syrups. Taking their place beside the Gin Cocktail we suddenly start seeing more imaginative drinks such as the Japanese Cocktail, Saratoga Cocktail, Morning Glory Cocktail, and the Manhattan Cocktail. The bartender, free to express their talents in a culinary fashion, began to devise new and exciting drinks. This evolution is perhaps best shown by looking at the updated 1887 edition of Jerry Thomas' *BarTenders Guide*. While his 1862 edition buried its ten different cocktail recipes behind other mixed drink categories, the 1887 edition proudly moved it to the very front of the book, and doubled its number to twenty. In 1895, George J. Kappeler published *Modern American Drinks*, which lists 75 different recipes for drinks labeled as "cocktails". While four of these drinks were essentially non-alcoholic (Clam Cocktail, Clam Juice Cocktail, Oyster Cocktail, Soda Cocktail), it still represents the boost that cocktails were attaining during this time.

While earlier cocktails were simply variations on the spirit, sugar, water, bitters theme, we now start seeing recipes, which are experimenting with adding small amounts of complex flavored liqueurs in order to tease out different nuances from the overall flavor profile. One such drink that is included in *Modern American Drinks* is the Ford Cocktail:

FORD COCKTAIL.
Three dashes benedictine, three dashes orange bitters,
half a jigger Tom gin, half a jigger French vermouth. Mix in

Here we see a very early use of Benedictine as a cocktail ingredient. Benedictine was intended to be taken straight, and was essentially considered to be a health restorative. You can compare its use in cocktails as being similar to using various spices in cooking. Originally, many of the spices we use today were primarily being used as either a medicinal additive, or more commonly as a way to mask the flavors of meats and vegetables which were going bad. Once the use of spices in cooking was being added purely for their flavor enhancing (as opposed to masking) abilities, we saw the culinary arts burst forth onto the scene. While Benedictine might have originally been designed for medicinal purposes, its secret recipe of various aromatics, fruit peels, and herbs, provided a complex flavor which could be artfully added as a cocktail ingredient in order to bring out some exciting flavor experiences.

In the late 1800s and early 1900s, by using diverse ingredients of higher quality than previously available, we finally see a strong awakening of the mixed drink in general, and the cocktail in specific. While it's inebriating properties were always readily apparent, there was at least recognition that perhaps, just perhaps, there was something more to this liquid cuisine.

The responsibility for driving the culinary achievements in cocktails of course rests firmly on the shoulders of the bartenders of the day. Their dedication, their knowledge, and the very passion with which they executed their duties formed the foundation for the drinks we may all take for granted today.

---

91. George J. Kappeler, *Modern American Drinks* (New York: Merriam Company, 1895), 31.

A bartender in those days was a combination of artist and scientist, who was looked upon with some awe by mere statesmen, bankers and leaders in other professions.[92]

It can be difficult to comprehend that even though it occurred just a little over a hundred years ago, there is really very little known of exactly how stringent or demanding the training regime for new bartenders would have been during the 1800s. Just as was true of most trades of the day however, the use of an apprenticeship program was most likely the common training methodology. This consisted of the "bar tender"-to-be (during that time the term was two separate words, not appearing as "bartender" until about 1882) taking a position as apprentice to the head bar tender. Depending on the establishment, they might work at that position for several years before being truly considered qualified to be a full fledged bar tender.

One could still see relics of earlier days at Harry Johnson's Little Jumbo saloon near Grant Street, which had a sign before the door dating back to the time when a bartender had to serve an apprenticeship of several years.[93]

The result of this training was a generation of bartenders who understood what it meant to create cocktails that embodied flavors beyond simply being a "mixed drink." Imagine the dedication that classically trained French chefs or pastry chefs apply to their craft, or even the long hours of study and selection that the sommelier puts into simply building their wine list and making recommendations to their customers. The bartenders of the late 1800s and early 1900s were cut from the same cloth, and practiced their art form with the same dedication and sense of accomplishment.

---

92. Henry Collins Brown, *In the Golden Nineties* (Valentine's Manual, Hastings-On-Hudson, 1928), 323.
93. Ibid.

The world of the bartender was one that was surrounded by grandeur and excellence. Bartenders would dress sharply and with supreme style, they would serve their cocktails in an elegantly diverse set of glassware, and the very bars from which they would hold court would often be large and impressive structures that formed the stage for the liquid cuisine that would be issued forth. In the 1880s, the rapidly growing market for ornate wooden bars caught the eye of the Brunswick Company, the same people famous for their billiard tables today. Soon, they began manufacturing amazingly ornate cathedrals to mixology, which are still the treasured centerpiece of bars around the world.

Just as leading chefs demand quality ingredients to go into the meals that they prepare, so too would bartenders pay specific attention to the use of quality spirits, liqueurs, mixers, and garnishes for use in their cocktails. Recipes of the day would never use sour mix, or any pre-mix shortcut simply to churn out drinks faster. Saving time or money at the expense of the cocktail that was produced was unheard of within any establishment that valued its reputation.

Suppose you need for your drink three or four ingredients; take every article genuine but one, and you will spoil the entire drink by the one that is not genuine.[94]

How does all of this translate into the modern bartender? How do cocktails today compare to those that were served only a hundred years ago? Unfortunately, somewhere along the way we appear to have lost our way. The blame, or at least most of it, can probably be laid at the feet of Prohibition. During that short period of time, with their profession essentially outlawed, bartenders effectively had only three choices. They could relocate to another country and continue their trade, they could stay in America and seek

---

94. William Schmidt, *The Flowing Bowl: When and What to Drink* (New York: Charles L. Webster & Co., 1892), 110.

a different profession, or they could become outlaws and try to work at underground saloons. Unfortunately, most of the bartenders of the day would put aside their mixing glasses, hang up their uniform, and take the prudent option of looking for other ways to make a living.

Today, we might look back at this time in history and read stories about the countless speakeasies of the day and think that they would have provided a perfect venue for these now out-of-work bartenders, unfortunately these establishments did not just spring up out of thin air, but took several years to gradually evolve out of the imposed structure of the situation. By the time they had a need for real bartenders, very few of them were still available. Those few that did make their way into such a position would most likely have found themselves short-changed by having to use products of questionable, if not downright perverse quality. The atmosphere of most of these establishments were turned up to such a degree as to prevent the customers from needing to pay too much attention to the quality of the beverages, that they included alcohol of one type or another was all that was required of them.

Coming out of Prohibition, America found itself in sudden need of an army of bartenders, bartenders who no longer existed. Those who had been working beneath the law were obvious choices, but they had spent far too long working with bathtub gin turning out poor excuses for cocktails to be able to suddenly turn into the culinary bartenders of pre-Prohibition. Other bartending positions would be filled by anybody who could hold a bottle and show up to work. Add to this the fact that America was still in the throws of the Depression, and you don't have a very good formula for encouraging restaurants to spend time, energy, and expense, on training or hiring the best and brightest bartenders.

With a well-stocked cocktail library of books that have been written since Prohibition, it is easy to consult the historical archive and see the process of how the art of the cocktail evolved, and just watch the recipes degrade across the decades into versions that are pale shadows of what they once were. Orange bitters, which were once the most common form of cocktail bitters, all but completely disappeared from the scene. The Martini, a culinary classic that was once an exquisitely well-balanced cocktail, has turned into simply a glass of cold booze. The Old Fashioned, perhaps the closest thing to the "original" cocktail, has been turned into little more than a poorly made whiskey spritzer, which I can't blame anybody for not wanting to order. And sour mix has become the ketchup of the industry, being used in countless drinks as a way to cover up the inexactitude of the modern bartender.

The process of training a bartender today is all but laughable. Sure, there are bartending schools of various sorts that make themselves available, but none that carry the same level of credentials and respect as the culinary academies that produce professional chefs. Some bars might think that they use an apprenticeship process as we would have seen in the 1800s, but more often than not they are simply sticking a former server behind the bar with some tattered and questionable book of recipes, and letting them learn the ropes in a trial-by-fire manner. Worst of all, is that for decades now we have had these untrained bartenders being the trainers of the bartenders working beneath them. Just watch the movie *Cocktail*, and you'll see the level of culinary enlightenment that this can provide.

An inexpert cook never will become an artist nor a chef de cuisine by simply reading a book on cookery, no matter by whom or how intelligently written, and no man can ever become an artist behind the bar by simply looking into this book or possessing it. A great deal of ingenuity and taste is required on the part of a chef in an important position, and the same is required on the part of a man in the capacity of a bartender.[95]

The common excuse I hear from bartenders as to why they might be making their drink in a particularly poor manner will often be simply "that's the way I learned it," or "that's the way we've always made it here," or "that's the way it's written in the book I use." Each of these is just a variation on a theme that puts all of the blame on whatever might have passed as their training, be it from book or practice. Clearly, such a bartender is not taking the initiative to actually study the craft, or to see if they could improve the quality of the products that they produce. Instead they take the easy route out and just memorize a wad-o-recipes and then play diligent host to the party of revelers that come through each day, and hope that they are able to score some good tips.

It is also common for the bartender to put the blame on the poor drinks that they produce on the customers that have come before. Perhaps it's as innocent as not using bitters in their Old Fashioned, shaking a Manhattan (instead of stirring it), or serving their Sidecars made with sour mix and served in an ice-filled pint glass. "That's how everybody seems to want them made," or something like it will be their alibi. Beneath that, is the often held sentiment that "the customer is always right", which will often be twisted to essentially put the customer in charge of their training, and just because a few customers might specifically ask to leave bitters out of their drink, they assume that this is how it should be done. What they are really doing is excusing them from the process, and admitting that they are no

---

95. William Schmidt, *The Flowing Bowl: When and What to Drink* (New York: Charles L. Webster & Co., 1892), 110.

longer playing the role of chef, but instead are playing the
role of puppet.

A bartender ought to be leading and not to be led. An actor must understand for himself how to amuse his audience and how to gain a reputation: he never would succeed by simply following another man's guidance.[96]

The products available to us today are far superior, and present a wider variety of options, than those that were in use by the bartenders of the 1800s, so it should be possible for us to create cocktails that can surpass the achievements of anything that they might have done. While it is impossible to actually try any of the drinks exactly as they would have been prepared by pre-Prohibition bartenders, it is fairly safe to assume that very few modern bartenders are currently producing cocktails which could come close to any of those.

What we need is a return of the passion of what it means to be a bartender; we need guidance, motivation, and opportunity. We need bartenders who can take their craft seriously and learn to appreciate their culinary role. We need restaurants that will place the same level of attention to the quality of products available from the bar, as they do to the products coming out of their kitchens. Similarly, we need customers who realize that the cocktail is far more than just an alcohol delivery vehicle, and that it is, rather, a form of liquid cuisine that can be treasured and appreciated just as any fine meal. We need to reflect upon the past, learn from it, and then re-build the art form.

Where once the only cocktail bitters easily available were Angostura, it is now common to also see Peychaud's bitters, as well as several different brands of orange bitters on the market. There are even several different bars—the Zig Zag Café in Seattle, the Pegu Club in New York, No.

---

96. William Schmidt, *The Flowing Bowl: When and What to Drink* (New York: Charles L. Webster & Co., 1892), 110.

9 Park in Boston, along with others—that have taken up the practice of using home-made bitters in several of their cocktails. This refreshing return of one of the products that was at the core of defining the very essence of a cocktail is a promising sign that changes are on the horizon.

The Brunswick Company no longer produces the bars upon which they earned their reputation. When they closed up that part of their business it was providing $4 million in annual sells, making up 25 percent of the companies business. The market for them fell out as the temperance movement gained momentum just prior to Prohibition, and they've never tried to go back. Today however this role has been taken up by the Wallace & Hinz Company,[97] that currently does only a fraction of the business which was once a cornerstone of the American bar, despite the fact that there is an order of magnitude more bars today, than there were back then.

Vintage cocktail books, which were once merely a curiosity, have turned into a popular business. Not only are copies of many of these older books fetching larger and larger sums when they happen to show up in used book stores or online auctions, but several of these books are being reprinted in faithful facsimile editions. One publishing company, New Day Publishing,[98] has reprinted Jerry Thomas' *The Bar Tender's Guide* from 1862, *The Old Waldorf-Astoria Bar Book* from 1935, and *The Stork Club Bar Book* from 1946. While such books may only provide a glimpse of how cocktails might have played a role in the past, the enthusiasm by which people are looking toward the past in this way is the first step in trying to restore some of our culinary history.

97. http://www.whbars.com
98. http://www.cocktailbooks.com

It is possible that by taking a careful look at what bartenders of the past were accomplishing we can provide a conduit for breathing life back into the culinary art of the cocktail by exposing people to its history, its potential. To fully bear fruit, the audience for this information needs to include restaurants, bars, bartenders, and even customers. Each of them plays a crucial role in bringing about a new appreciation of the cocktail as cuisine. More importantly, it is the role of those of us who already see this potential, and understand its historic significance, to do what we can to provide the necessary education and inspiration to stimulate the progress along this journey.

WHAT MAKES
A GREAT BAR?

BY DALE DEGROFF

*Dale DeGroff knows that a successful bar
survives on more than just bartenders
making fabulous cocktails. It takes tight
planning, organized management, and
dedication to the craft and the profession.
Here, he instills the wisdom he's learned
over the years along with a few stories of
what it takes to make a great bar.*

I **WAS TEACHING MY CLASS** called "Home Mixology" at the Institute of Culinary Education in New York and one of the participants asked me what makes a great bar. It wasn't the first time I was asked that question but as I began to answer with the standard...great drinks, great service...I stopped myself and decided to think a bit deeper before giving a formula answer. I know what makes a great drink, but what makes a great bar is not as tangible. Luck is part of it, planning and details thought out by a caring owner, sure, but bars develop a character of their own; some over time others almost as soon as they open.

PJ Clarke's in New York City has been a magnet for patrons from around the world for over half a century and a working bar since the nineteenth century. The walls are covered with paintings and photographs some of which haven't been touched in a hundred years. The dirt and dust stalactites that hung from the lights and shillelaghs behind the bar were finally dusted off when the place changed hands recently.

The Lavezzo family who owned Clarke's for years operated an antique shop above the bar when the current owner put it on the market in 1948. Young Danny Lavezzo decided he would like to run the place and they took over the business that year. The timing was right. The war was over and United States was sailing full steam ahead into a booming economy; everyone was in the mood for a good time! Almost overnight the place was packed. Danny had a way with people and he believed that you don't make money by locking the doors so he remained open every hour of every day that the law would allow—365 days a year, only closing at four in the morning to sweep and mop for a couple hours. Clarke's became the ultimate nightcap destination in a city that just didn't want to go to sleep.

In the height of Clarke's popularity, Frank Sinatra had his own table and used a separate entrance on the 55th street side of the building that entered directly into the dining room to avoid walking through the bar. The back room was the inner sanctum. In my first ten years as a Clarke's patron, I never made it to the back room. Even if I had made it I couldn't have afforded to tip the maitre'd, let alone pay the check!. During baseball season the tables were peppered with players and umps. If there was a movie premier or a Broadway opening, Richard Burton and Peter O'Toole might be in the middle of a drinking contest.

I was a front bar customer and that suited me fine. Across from the bar was a sandwich counter where some claim the first hamburgers in the United States were served, which, like most bar lore, was just bravado. But they were good! Those little babies came off the grill incognito on a paper plate with a large slice of onion hiding under the bun; but the meat was the best available on the market and they were cooked to perfection. There was a hamburger stand across from the bar in the front room and no one with any class left the back or the front room without laying a tip on the hamburger man...he did almost as well as the waiters! And no one ordered just the burger because the chef made the most amazing crispy home fried potatoes, and a real Caesar Salad.

Frank Conefry was one of the mainstays behind the front bar in those days and lore had it that in the 1960s and 1970s he was bringing down a princely $500 a night. He built a church in his hometown in Ireland, so they said! The place was so crowded that two bouncers were stationed on either side of the door like the Pillars of Hercules wearing sport coats two sizes too small to emphasize their powerful presence. A troublemaker was flanked on both sides by

these gentle giants and deposited on the sidewalk before
he knew what was up.

The place would suddenly become electric as the word spread instantly that Sinatra, or Judy Garland, or Lauren Bacall, or all three, had slid in the back entrance. The front bar regulars would look bored by the news—so what's the big deal—while the neophytes could barely control their bladders!

The first fancy bar and grill I experienced was the original Charlie O's in Rockefeller Center. It was 1967 or '68, and I was in town for the New Year to join the crunch in Times Square, it was actually fun then; no metal pens to isolate the revelers and open containers were tolerated, the bars were even open and making lots of dough! Today New Years Eve in Times Square is a choreographed Orwellian nightmare in a barren wasteland of shuttered restaurants and bars. No booze allowed or eats because bags of any kind are prohibited and taking a leak is out of the question.

Charlie O's was a Restaurant Associates creation when Joe Baum was at the helm. He had a wonderfully creative team behind him working on the concept from Lois, Holland, and Callaway Advertising. It was Joe's most successful bar, next to the Promenade Bar at the Rainbow Room. It was a perfect example of a great New York bar and grill.

Charley O's had a long bar of dark mahogany along the east wall with beautiful oval windows looking out on Rockefeller Plaza and 48th street. Just inside the door on the right was the smaller sandwich bar with the great turkey and roast beef and brisket as well as big bowls of soused shrimp, etc. Eamon worked the sandwich bar on and off for years. He took time off every couple years to get rich in some scheme or other but always returned and was always welcome.

Ron Holland and George Lois worked very closely with Joe Baum on the concept for Charley O's, as they did for many of Joe's creations like La Fonda del Sol, Tower Suite, Forum of the Twelve Caesars, Zum Zum, Windows on the World, and even the magnificent failures like Spats with its marvelous address 33 West 33rd street! Ron and George chose the pictures and captions that covered the walls at Charley O's and they were so successful that people would bring friends to the place for a drink just to take a walk-through tour of the pictures. Quotes like George Jean Nathan quipping " I only drink to make other people interesting," or Harpo Marx's classic line: "…_____…" lined the walls. One featured Abraham Lincoln in a Brady photograph standing in front of a battlefield command tent with several senior officers delivering his famous defense of General Grant's drinking habits, "Find out what General Grant drinks and send a case of it to my other generals!"

It was a wonderful hang out, a bar for everyone; gamblers, ad men, writers, politicians, and gangsters. Every Year Pat Moynihan threw his St. Paddy's breakfast at Charley O's. I worked many St Paddy's breakfasts as part of the Irish Coffee crew; we started at one end of the bar like an assembly line—one bartender pouring whiskey and brown sugar syrup, followed by the coffee man and then the hand whipped, unsweetened cream. We would work our way down the bar and when we reached the end we started all over again. This went on non-stop from 6:00 A.M. for the rest of the day. It was at one of these St. Paddy's breakfasts that Bobby Kennedy announced his candidacy for president of the United States.

In 1974 I finished my lunch shift as a waiter when the day manager ran through the dining room just frantic. Her name was Marcy Bloom and I will always be in her debt. Peter Ashkenazi the current owner of Charley O's had the contract to cater the parties at the mayors residence based on his fathers large contributions to all the candidates running for mayor. This particular party was a biggie because Mayor Beame was presenting the keys of the city to Rupert Murdoch who had just bought the *New York Post*. The bartender for the party didn't show and Marcy asked whether any of the waiters knew how to tend bar. I lied and announced that I was a bartender.

I ran over to the bar with a pencil and index card and quizzed Mike Flynn, an Irish bartender, on how to make several drinks, which I wrote down quickly. I dashed off to Gracie Mansion. As it turned out, the most difficult drink I had to make was a gin and tonic.

So,...WHAT REALLY MAKES A GREAT BAR?

What drew the crowd back again and again to Charlie O's? Below are some of the tangible elements.

SURROUNDINGS OF SUBSTANCE

This doesn't mean expensive and highly designed, although some great bars are...but a neighborhood joint can have surroundings of substance. My first neighborhood bar in NYC was Paddy McGlades, a one hundred-year-old gem on the corner of 68th and Columbus across the street from ABC News and an ABC soap opera studio. The ceiling was mahogany that framed beautifully painted glass squares. They were painted from the inside, so even as they aged and peeled the effect was enhanced. Over the bar among the shillelaghs and right above the old National Cash Register was a blow-up of a race track photo-finish of a triple heat to win at Aqueduct Race Track. The photograph from the sixties was a gift to Al "the Bishop," a bartender for thirty-five years, from the ABC news crew that used McGlades as their living room. The beveled glass mirrors reflected a big round institutional clock with the number backwards so you could read the time in the mirror without turning around. On the wall across the room from the bar an artist and long time patron painted a marvelous mural that included many of the long time regulars and employees and even a special race horse Al won a load betting on. The mural was so wonderful that when the place closed (ABC was going to tear the building down then changed their mind) and became a Starbucks—moan—they left part of the mural on the wall.

A Proprietor

The owner, or partner, or even a long time trusted employee who is a presence, can fill this role. He sets the tone of the place. I don't mean mister hail fellow well met—there is staff hired for that, just a presence that the regulars can nod to across the room, and point out to the neophytes "there's the owner." Once in a while he does the right thing by a table of regulars. His being there makes everything work better…the staff for example. When they see the owner's passion, watch him bus a table or seat a guest that involvement inspires the staff and they give more to the place in a hundred different ways, almost adopting a proprietary feeling about the place. I remember sitting in PJ Clarks years ago and pointing out the owner Danny Lavezzo and telling the stories about his legendary bets at the track and about the easy way he had with everyone from Frank Sinatra to the Chinese busboy on duty.

The Bartender

The man who makes you to stay too long and come back everyday. That is the job in a nutshell. It is the why that is the secret. His drinks are good and he is fast, while still being a part of conversations up and down the bar, about everything under the sun from sports scores, to a restaurant location, to a pep-talk for an out of work pal. He opens and closes the place, handles the money, tips out the staff. If the owner sets the tone, the bartender projects it to the clientele. The bar is the engine of the place and the bartender is the engineer. The bartender is lots of things to lots of different people, and the person who does that job has to be at peace with that role and secure in his/her own identity.

Please don't be discouraged by all my stories of what used to be. I am very optimistic about the future of the cocktail bar business! In New York City alone we are experiencing a renaissance of great cocktail bars. And in cities around the country and around the world there is a community of talented and passionate bartenders dedicated to innovation and excellence. These wonderful oases of style, flavor and class, are not great or legendary yet...but they are well on the way to a serious shot at the triple crown.

So how do you open a joint and turn it into an institution? Well no guarantees but remember the concepts above and follow the practical steps below and you can stack the odds in your favor.

THE ANATOMY
OF THE CLASSIC COCKTAIL BAR

FUNDING

Raise enough money to stay open a year covering expenses without profit. When writing a business plan figure out the worst possible scenario and go with that. Find out if former tenants had trouble with their Certificate of Occupancy; remember you cannot do business without it. Investigate all applicable codes and have a meeting with a representative from the fire department before signing the lease. When you borrow try to avoid too many equity partners. These financial and real estate issues are really the whole ball of wax; some people luck into good situations but that is definitely the exception. Find a landlord willing to waive rent for a period during the build-out. Careful and detailed budgeting is paramount to success. I don't pretend to be expert in this area, but below are some budget considerations that must not be overlooked to write a successful business plan. Determine monthly expenses figuring the following:

- Bank loans
- Non-equity investors
- Equity investors
- Build-out
  —Watch out here, multiply the contractor's estimate by two.
  —Designer and architect fees
  —Appliances and refrigeration costs
- Liquor license
  —Secure a license before proceeding with all else.
  —If the license is existing, check to see if it is clear or if there are outstanding invoices form purveyors, these could add up to lots of money.
- Insurance, property, and liability
  —Bring in a pro to consult for sufficient liability
- Utilities
  —Get some history form previous tenants or the landlord
  —Heat and AC can be large expenses
- Payroll and payroll taxes
- Revenue taxes and property taxes, if they apply
- China, glass, and silver
- Linens, if applicable
- Opening liquor and food order
  —Determine a permanent store inventory and the cost to maintain for liquor, food, and dry goods
- Extras/misc. expenses.

The Design

Form without function, like style without substance, is profoundly frustrating and will ultimately lead to failure.

The bars that date to the nineteenth century often combined design with function much more successfully then modern bars do. One undeniable aspect of Clarke's, like many of the nineteenth century bars that used to line First, Second, and Third Avenues in New York City, is creature comfort. The height of the bar and the bar stools, the brass foot rail, the rounded arm rest at the front edge of the bar top, and the mirrors behind the bar that allow bar patrons to monitor the activity up and down the bar, were all features in these bars that combined with efficient production facilities and surroundings of substance to make sitting at the bar such a pleasure.

I don't want to recreate the nineteenth-century bar look! I just want the twenty-first century bar to function. Don't let designers make decisions about the bar design. A cocktail bar is as specialized as a kitchen. Kitchens are designed by chefs to produce a specific cuisine and so a bar should be designed with the end production in mind. The chef is the first person hired when starting a restaurant and so the head bartender or beverage manager or both should come on the payroll, at least partially, early on in the planning of the project.

There are some classic bar features that must be present for simple creature comfort. A bar should always have a foot rail; a bar without a foot rail is uncomfortable, the foot always searching for a perch. The stools must be comfortable and also have a perch for the foot at the same height. Under bar knee space is an obvious design feature that is too often missing leaving guests perching side-saddle on the stool with knees constantly banging the bar facing. The width of the bar top is critical to good communication and simple good service. In Europe I continually find myself at a bar so wide the bartender cannot reach the outer edge of the bar for simple service and cleaning!

Bars that are built too high or too low are a problem. I've encountered this more in Europe than in the United States; Follow these guidelines they have worked for one hundred and fifty years and still provide maximum comfort and efficient bar service:

- Perfect bar height is 42 inches.
- The stool has to fit the bar and must also have a foot perch built into the design.
- Foot rail 6 to 8 inches off the floor and 8 inches from the bar die
- There should be 24 inches of linear space along the bar allotted for each stool.
- The ideal width of the bar between the bartender and the patron is 24 inches including the drip rail; this permits the bartender to reach to the outside edge of the bar for service and provides a comfortable expanse for the guest.
- Too many bars don't allow enough space for the knees to fit under the bar when seated! The "T" shaped affair made up of the bar top and the bar die that supports the bar top, should meet very specific measurements. The guest side of the bar die should allow 14 inches for leg room under the bar
- The inner edge of the bar top should have a drip rail 3.5 inches wide. These rails are practical catching the spill from a guest drink before it ends in the ice or fruit or whatever else the bartender has on the under bar counter.
- Under bar sinks, ice bins and counters should all be stainless steel and mounted on legs that raise them off the floor 12 inches for easy access for floor cleaning. But not so high that

access to sinks, under bar counters, and ice bins is impeded by the over-hang of the bar top.

- The back bar should be the same height as the front bar.

These simple common sense measurements are the first step towards a workable bar that is also comfortable for the guest.

Bars are so often straight lines with guests lined up side-by-side along the bar. In the nineteenth century they discovered how to create communication between guests lined up at the bar. Below the ubiquitous reclining nude there was always a long mirror in which the guest seated at the bar could keep tabs on comings and goings in the room, see people down the length of the bar, and enjoy the general scene as it unfolded throughout the night.

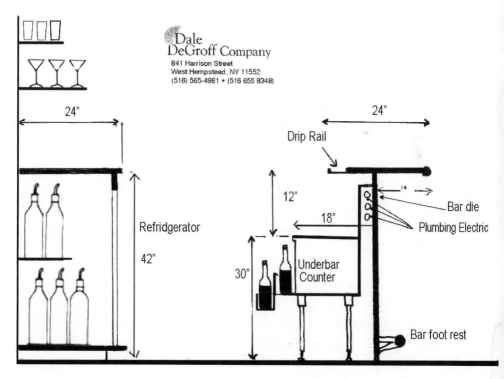

Dale DeGroff Company
841 Harrison Street
West Hempstead, NY 11552
(516) 565-4981 • (516) 655 8348

Specifications for the ideal bar. (Copyright 2006. Dale DeGroff.)

To complete the design from a production standpoint we must look at the equipment behind the bar and how it is arranged. A classic shaker bar that is intended to produce shaken cocktails for large numbers of guests needs special features. Each bar station must be like a cockpit with the following features:

- A working sink with drain boards on both sides. The sinks must be deep enough for continually rinsing cocktail shakers.
- An ice bin with divisions to accommodate cubed and crushed ice and a division to chill juices
- Speed racks, even double if possible attached to the ice bin and drain boards
- Refrigeration within easy reach behind the bartender
- Additional spirits within reach on the back bar for cordials and call brands
- Easy access to sodas either bottled (which I prefer) or from a gun
- Glass froster (one for each two stations) this is not a luxury but as necessary as a plate warmer is to the hot line in the kitchen
- A minimum of four sets of cocktail shakers and strainers per station (I prefer the Boston shaker sets)
- Shelves with glassware within reach
- A blender station
- If glasses are washed behind the bar one washer for each two stations
- Waste drop adjacent to bar station

Finally all these features must be within close proximity of the bartender so he can produce ninety percent of the drinks without taking more than two steps in any direction.

A large property with lots of lounge seating should have a separate service bar station designed in the back of the house. A lounge that seats more than 80 guests needs a separate service bar and may need more than one service bartender. Specialty drinks that are handmade in front of the guest at the main bar can be made in batches to expedite the service to large numbers of guests but that requires special design features. Batch drinks made in gallon pour-n-store containers need additional refrigeration. The server area must have a glassware station, ice bin, soda supply, and counter space for several set-ups at once, coffee station and refrigeration. The server should be able to completely set up their trays with glasses, ice and coffee and soft drinks while they wait for service.

TIME TO RE-THINK BAR ACCESSORIES

In Europe I have seen an innovation that is brilliant. Instead of those silly and ugly plastic or stainless garnish trays we still insist on using, bars have refrigerated drawers adjacent to the ice bin on the right or left for each station. The drawers contain the wide variety of garnish necessary to produce the exotic drinks that have become the trademark of the London style bar: berries of all kinds, traditional garnishes of lemon, lime, etc., also melon, herbs, and much more. Consider, for example, providing a cold garnish in a cold drink. What a concept? I can't count the number of Martinis I have had that have been instantly spoiled by the addition of three large heat bombs skewered on a pick and dropped into my drink by a well meaning bartender who just never thought it out!

The genius of Sasha Petraske who operates Milk and Honey and now the East Side Company in New York City is that he never was a bar guy before deciding to open one and he approached each problem with fresh eyes and more importantly common sense!

Cocktails can be successfully batched and still be fresh and lively if certain rules are followed. Let me use the most popular cocktail of the last several years to illustrate—the Cosmopolitan. Batch the non-volatile ingredients—in this case the cranberry juice, the citrus vodka, and the Cointreau or triple sec—in the correct proportions in a gallon store-n-pour for storage. During service at the service bar pour the batch over into either pitchers or quart size store and pour containers for use. Depending on the pour size and glass size at your operation pour between 3 and 4 ounces of the batch mix into a shaker and add the fresh lime juice (the volatile ingredient) at the point of sale. The bartender grabs two ingredients instead of four. In my years at the Rainbow Room we batched several complex drinks in order to keep them on the menu; some, like the Singapore Sling and the Planters Punch, we batched permanently for the whole twelve years!

The Staff: How to Hire, How to Train

If a bar owner gets it all right in the design and the build-out but makes a bad hire or doesn't train staff properly all can be lost.

The demand for well-made new and classic cocktails is so great these days that bar and restaurant owners are realizing that these cocktail programs don't take care of themselves...they have to be managed just like the kitchen. That means creating a position similar to "Executive Chef" to oversee the cocktail program. Find a person who shares your vision and work with them to hire a staff that does, too.

That person may be a bartender/manager or a full time beverage manager. Smaller operations may not have the resources to create a new management position and will opt for a combined position. A good solution is a general manager with a passionate interest in the beverage side of

the business. Passion is definitely the key to success when
hiring. Sometimes hiring for experience alone is a mistake.
With a little experience but a lot of drive an intelligent
person will progress rapidly with good training.

Depending on the personnel, an outside training consultant may be required at first. The initial training must be
extensive. The following is a good outline that highlights
areas to cover:

- **History of the Cocktail and the Bartending Profession**
  Lecture and presentation on the history of the cocktail and
  a look at the profession of bartending—how it has evolved
  and where it is presently headed. (Vintage cocktail books
  and bartending tools are good helps for this section of the
  training.)
- **Tool Handling, Techniques, and Garnish Preparation**
  What are the tools necessary for the preparation of great
  cocktails and how to handle them. Demonstration and review of technique; shaking, stirring, and rolling drinks, and
  preparing drinks with showmanship and finesse. Garnish
  preparation and management; a great cocktail bar requires
  much more than standard garnish.
- **Recipe Preparation**
  Hands-on drinks preparation with the staff; focus on the
  menu drinks specifically with all the bartenders preparing
  all the cocktails. Overview: Cocktail preparation, recipe
  knowledge, etc.
- **Spirit Categories and Classics**
  A four-session lecture and presentation exploring spirit cat-
  egories; their history, how they are made, tasting of different
  styles within the category, and hands on drink preparation
  of the classics from each of the categories:
  I. White Spirits Gin and Vodka
  II. Whiskies of the World
  III. Brandies and Liqueurs
  IV. South of the Border: Rum, Tequila, Mezcal, and
  Cachaça
- **Service Dynamics**

The relationship, or contract, between a server and a guest in the dining room is clear. The guest, in effect, rents the table for the duration of the meal. Close attention to the needs at the table is paramount, but the privacy of the space must not be violated by the service. The server in the dining room is always an interloper at the table and must get the job done quickly and unobtrusively. Not so for the bartender. The guest at the bar is in a shared space and the bartender sets the tone of that space. Even, if a guest is short or less than cordial, the bartender, according to the contract, cannot respond in kind. If a guest is unruly to the extent that the other guests suffer or are endangered, immediate action, usually by senior management, is obviously required. Once a bartender becomes unpleasant, rude, or morose, in reaction to a guest, a gratuity, or whatever, the shared space is compromised and people will leave. It is a one-sided contract, weighted in favor of the guest, but in practice it is an opportunity for the bartender to do what he was hired to do best, turn difficult guests into friends, make great drinks, and even, on occasion, teach people how to have a good time.

Bartenders need to sharpen their powers of observation and highly develop their ability to listen. In the first encounter with a guest, the bartender will determine not only the drink, but also the mood of the guest. Determine if conversation is welcome; more generally, why has the guest come; determine how to make the visit a success.

The skill a bartender has in handling the tools and the small theatrical elements, such as the flaming of citrus peels, can return huge dividends. Not a circus act, but a sense of confidence that is apparent to a guest at the bar. A bartender is most definitely on stage. That scrutiny also exposes the bartender's grooming habits and demands that he be carefully groomed down to the fingernails!

A bartenders skill and cleverness at being many things to many people is one of the most compelling and challenging aspects of the job. The bartender is a source of information on the day's events in sports and general news, a glossary of where to dine, drink, and see and be seen. He has the ability to keep peace in a light handed way, to gently separate a gentle man from a lady who may not find his company as compelling as he finds hers'. Rudeness to a bar guest is never acceptable, there are too many alternate ways of reacting to a difficult guest. Even the most difficult of guests can be handled with a professional demeanor, and sometimes help is required.

EMPOWER YOUR EMPLOYEES

Treat your bartenders like professionals; viewing them as craftsmen promotes that image. Meet with them regularly to discuss menu changes, new products, beverage policies, and problems with execution. Let the bartenders, through the head bartender, have input in the decisions that effect their work.

- Choice of product: Special drinks call for a wide range of products, make sure the bartender has what he needs.
- Seasonal menu changes: when bartenders are qualified, let them participate in the seasonal menu changes. In larger operations, input needs to be channeled through their supervisors, but be sure that this input is considered when changes are made.
- Choice of glassware: Great cocktails need correct glassware, do the research and be sure you have the glass for the drink.
- Wine by the glass program: Maintaining an extensive wine by the glass program can have disastrous financial consequences if it is not properly managed. Determine how much

to open for a service, how will the wine be stored after opening, and, most important, establish a system to move the
wine once it is open. Maybe a blackboard system, or something similar, to keep the information in front of the servers
as the evening goes on so they can sell the open wine.

- Managing garnish: Fresh fruit is another huge expense, and
most bars over-cut garnish and end up tossing out lots of
lemon and lime wedges. Also get creative with garnish,
flame the orange and lemon peels, it is a great show and will
make the bar special.

EQUIPMENT

Supply a clean well-equipped work place. Do the
bartenders have the equipment they need to do their job
well? If the bar is serious about shaken cocktails, then
every station needs four sets of shakers. Figure out what
equipment you need for your operation and be sure that
the bars are well outfitted.

OTHER RESOURCES

Subscribe to industry publications that keep the staff
current on trends in cocktails and wine. Bring in industry
guests; the spirit purveyors you work with can bring brand
managers and distillers to your premises for seminars.
Encourage research and development that include local
specialties, local products, famous local places, bars, restaurants, food traditions, and beers.

FRESH INGREDIENTS

"Fresh Juices!...Bartenders Have done it for one hundred
years...If you can't figure it out I will find someone who
can." Joe Baum's encouragement to me when I tentatively
volunteered that some back-up sour mix might be necessary in busy times.

Without exception, drinks that employ fresh lemon and lime juice require more training and attention than any other single category of cocktail. This is because the delicate balance between sweet and sour is hard to achieve, and because the range of guest preference is broad and makes special demands on a bartenders powers of observation. Sweet and sour drinks have a smaller window of acceptability and an error of less than a quarter ounce in either direction when using fresh lemon or lime juice is unacceptable and can render a drink undrinkable

Here are steps that make it easier to implement and maintain a successful fresh juice program. Most bars in the United States and in the UK have access to purveyors who sell very acceptable quality fresh-squeezed orange and grapefruit juice by the gallon or half gallon. As these are not pasteurized, they will spoil rapidly without proper handling. They must be delivered cold, put away immediately, and kept refrigerated until used.

Remember also that fruit juice is an agricultural product and so is affected by growing conditions. Too much rain can produce juice that is watery and tart. (I am not above a little dosage to bring the juice around to where it needs to be to make my cocktails taste right!)

On the other hand, fresh squeezed lemon and lime juice are not as successful when purchased instead of prepared in-house. The problem is twofold. First the commercial juicing machines often grind into the white pithy portion of the fruit, resulting in an unacceptably high percentage of the bitter pith in the juice. When the juice is thawed—these products are usually frozen to extend shelf life—the juice will have a layer of white milky substance at the bottom. When shaken, the pith goes into the solution, rendering the juice too bitter for proper cocktails. Second, lemon and lime juice, because they don't have the sugar content of orange and grapefruit to help preserve them, have a shorter shelf life of about 24 hours, and commercially squeezed juice, frozen or not, will always be beyond that threshold.

How to Make It Happen

When you make the leap and decide fresh juice is the way to go, the following steps will prove a valuable guide.

If your point of sale system will allow it, review the last six months of sales to determine how many sour style drinks you are selling. It will give you a starting point to determine the amounts of fresh juice you will need. Remember that a commercial sour mix is sugar, water, flavoring, and preservatives, and drinks made with the sour mix are one shot of spirit and the rest is the mix—a drink like a Whiskey Sour or a Collins will require about two ounces of the stuff! Fresh juice, on the other hand, is concentrated. Drinks made with fresh juice seldom use more than three quarters of an ounce, so usage will differ dramatically! This information, along with the actual yields from squeezing the fresh fruit, will help you and the food and beverage controller determine the costs of the drinks made with fresh fruit.

Meet with the Purchasing Department, as first they need to get with the grocery purveyor to find the proper lemons and limes for juicing. The lemons that come in 169- to 200-count boxes are small and full of juice. The low-box-count lemons, say 95-count, etc., are fancy, thick skinned, and have very little juice—they are for garnish only. Limes are easier to purchase, but the rule of thumb is that the thin skinned, smaller fruit generally has much more juice and is cheaper. A 200-count box of lemons will yield, on average, two-and-a-half liters of fresh juice. Limes can vary by season dramatically, but the average is about three quarters of an ounce per lime.

Next step is a training session with bartenders and bar backs. Managers or supervisors need to be present for all training sessions. Outline the program from beginning to end and have everyone taste the drinks made with fresh juice against drinks made with the mix; the logic of the change will become very clear to all.

Purchase a Sunkist commercial juicer, very efficient and very powerful, or a similar commercial juicer. The bar-back or bartender, or whoever is assigned to squeeze the juice, should pull the fruit for the following day the night before and leave it overnight at room temperature. Cold fruit is stingy and will cut the output by a third. When squeezing the juice use a fine kitchen strainer, like a chinois, to remove the pulp. This is not breakfast, cocktails will look better without the pulp, and the pulp will dry on the inside of glasses, so glassware washing will be a nightmare if you don't strain. Straining will also allow the use of bottles and speed pourers to dispense the juice. I used glass pitchers at the Rainbow Room they were elegant but required extra attention in handling.

The person responsible for juicing must be trained to distinguish between the proper fruit for juicing and for garnish. Improper usage can be very costly. The amounts they squeeze must be determined by the flow of business on different days. Fresh juice can be used for three services, lunch, dinner, and the following lunch, but only if it is constantly under refrigeration. After three services it must be discarded.

The bartenders cannot keep the juice on the speed rack; it must be refrigerated. The lunch bartender should use the juice from the night before and then dispose of it after lunch. The new batch should be delivered after lunch to avoid mixing. Lunch usage will be low in most cases anyway. If there is consistently juice left at the lunch service of the following day you are over producing. The amounts must be reviewed as overproduction is very expensive.

The final and most important aspect of the program is training the bartenders in the recipes that employ the fresh juice. This includes training them how to use and prepare simple syrup. I recommend simple syrup at 50 brix (half sugar and half water). At the Rainbow Room, as busy as we were, we never used more then five or six litters of simple syrup per bar, per night. We could prepare another liter in the bottle in four minutes if we ran out during service. Simply fill the bottle half way with sugar and then to the top with water. Cork the bottle, turn it upside down and shake until the sugar is dissolved. If there is still some sediment of sugar after a few minutes rest, give it another quick shake and it is ready for immediate use, no cooking or cooling needed.

The lemon and lime juice is so concentrated, compared to sour mix, most bartenders are prone to overuse it. This brings up an issue I mentioned in the beginning. People do not come to a bar not to drink…so in the event that you prepare a sour style drink for someone and they just don't drink it, you should ask if there is a problem, and then fix it. Try this formula, I found it very successful for years in pleasing most of the public:

0.75 part sour
I part sweet
1.5 to 2 parts strong

For example, for a Whiskey Sour the recipe would be:

0.75 part lemon juice
I part simple syrup
1.5 to 2 parts whiskey
NOTE: I use parts because glass size will
determine the amount of the parts.

Training the bar staff to produce consistent drinks requires constant follow through by managers. Unless the bar requires all ingredients to be measured (damn near impossible with sour style drinks in a high volume business), sour style drinks should be assembled in the mixing glass half of the Boston Shaker in the following order:

- Juice
- Sweetener (simple syrup or triple sec or whatever)
- Dashes flavorings, etc...
- Base spirit
- Ice last

Use the mixing-glass half of the Boston Shaker to assemble ingredients—it is critical to see the ingredients in the glass. Require the bartenders to train using jiggers, paying strict attention to: 1) Where the juice comes on the side of mixing glass, 2) and then where the fill line is for the sweetener. These two ingredients will establish the balance of the drink.

After practicing this with jiggers, begin eyeballing the pour; by adding the ice last, the bartender can see on the side of the mixing glass where those first two critical ingredients fall, as well as the remaining ingredients. Don't let glass size drive your recipe—just the opposite! Choose a glass size that makes sense for the drink as costed out in your specs; an over-size glass will always lead to over pouring. It is the nature of the bartender to give the guest an impression of value and a partially filled oversized martini glass does not say "value" to the customer.

Pre-mix Fresh Sour

Some bars like to pre-mix a fresh sour mix, but unless you do two--one for lime and one for lemon–this presents problems. I want lemon-based drinks like a Collins, a Fizz, or a Sour, to taste like lemon, and lime-based drinks, like Daiquiris and Margaritas, to taste like lime. Stick with lemon, lime, and simple syrup; it is a time-honored practice that really works.

THE MAGIC

What really makes a joint great in the end analysis is the people who walk through the door day after day. They define and re-define the place from day to day and from year to year. They are what draw me to the job and to the long list of bars I visit over and over, as well as the longer list I have to visit before I run out of time. Cheers! Turn the lights off when you leave.

Raising the Bar on the High Seas

DEVELOPING AND MAINTAINING
SIGNATURE COCKTAIL PROGRAMS

BY RYAN MAGARIAN

Consistency in developing a mulit-venue bar operation is the challenge Ryan Magarian faced when he was commissioned by Holland America Line to revamp its program. He tells his tale here loaded down with tips that apply even to a single venue program.

WITH A GROWING PUBLIC interest and understanding of mixed drinks, namely hand crafted cocktails, as an integral part of the greater dining/culinary experience, signature drink programs are fast becoming de rigueur in the world's best restaurants, hotels, trendy nightspots, and now cruise lines.

Unfortunately, this growing excitement is forcing many bars and operations to attempt to "run before they can walk" in order to keep up with current trends, leaving them vulnerable to long term inconsistencies and, in many cases, inevitable failure. Over the past few years, I have continued to see more and more innovation in cocktail menus without the necessary program foundation to secure their quality, consistency, and long term success.

As a professional beverage/cocktail consultant, my value is in insuring that this is carefully avoided. I work to ensure that my clients' cocktail menus hit the mark with their guests, achieve a high level of innovation, attain fiscal success, and, importantly, that they remain consistent long after I am gone.

In sharing with you my time at sea with Holland America Line, I hope to offer some insight into how I have approached the development of detailed cocktail programs and offer evidence that, yes, these programs can operate fluidly and consistently even in the largest corporate environment.

One of my continuing frustrations in our industry is the lack of consistency in overall product quality when it comes to the modern bar experience.

Our current landscape does hold a few gems, though, namely the program at the Bellagio Resort and Casino. For those who aren't familiar with what is happening out there in the desert, upon opening the Bellagio, Steve Wynn showed some truly exciting foresight by bringing in mixologist Tony Abou-Ganim to ensure a first-class cocktail experience for his guests. It is my understanding that Tony not only put them on the right track with a cocktail program focused on beautifully rendered classics, and classic twists, made exclusively (and meticulously) with fresh juices and premium spirits, but also conducted lengthy and ongoing trainings and daily spot checks to ensure standards were met.

Unfortunately, the Bellagio seems to be an anomaly. Most large cocktail programs fail because of a lack of cohesive program vision, training, proper tools and ingredients, bad managerial support, a lack of motivated and knowledgeable staff, and, generally, the absence of systems of accountability. Further, it is apparent that in a restaurant environment the bar remains an afterthought to kitchen operations and design concerns, when, to ensure success, it should have equal attention. Now, attempting to implement this program for Holland America Line's entire fleet has allowed me to put my ideas to the test, and find out exactly what it takes to deliver consistently memorable cocktail experiences to cruisers in a very large, complex—and floating mind you—corporate environment.

Holland America Line, or HAL for short, has a proud heritage and holds a fleet of thirteen (fourteen. this winter) of the world's finest luxury ocean-going vessels. They range in size from cruisers that hold upwards of 2,000 passengers, down to the small but proud MS *Prinsendam* that travels the world, yearly, with its precious cargo of just under 800 passengers.

Over the past several years HAL has rolled out an all encompassing system of upgrades, termed "Signature of Excellence," that will totally refocus their efforts to ensure their position as the world's premier five-star cruise experience. It is a synergistic program designed to thoroughly analyze each area of a cruiser's experience and make necessary improvements. The Signature of Excellence program has also given a "green light" to an ultra-premium signature cocktail program, proving that HAL is willing to go the extra mile with total attention to detail and an ongoing commitment to the total guest experience.

Not to mention putting me to work....

And So It Begins

Development

Like most projects, this job—passion that pays is more like it—began with program brainstorming and cocktail development. Working with Kathy Casey Food Studios™ in Seattle, WA (through which I gained this opportunity), I am fortunate to have access to an amazing virtual kitchen and bar for recipe development. I spend a large portion of my paid time in this facility. More importantly, working side by side with Kathy and her team of talented chefs has really helped me understand complex flavor pairings and operational guidelines. This experience also helped me understand that success really is in the details, and this "chef-like" attention to detail really begins in the conception of the menu and in recipe creation.

For best results, the recipe development must be precise. Drinks are created using precise measurements and the recipes are then recorded in the same manner a chef would record a recipe in the kitchen.

The ingredients, whenever possible, should be fresh, the glassware suitable yet unique, and the garnishes should be appropriate and memorable.

HAL not only has a wide range of clientele, but the most varied and unique itineraries of any cruise line on Earth.

Just as each and every client expects varied and unique experiences from their cruise, the cocktail menu must be approached dynamically. As much as I would love to drop Corpse Revivers and Blood and Sands all over the high seas, it would be no more than a selfish endeavor lacking any direct benefit for my clients. We settled on sixty cocktails in five focused areas we thought our clients would understand, possibly be challenged by, but most certainly enjoy during their time at sea. They are "Tropical Specialties" (fresh Mojitos, Margaritas, and Spiced Daiquiris), "Citrus Signatures" (a wide selection of hand shaken citrus-style cocktails using hand-pressed fruits, herbs, and the occasional cucumber), "Oceanside Retro Favorites" (these are my personal favorites, including a grapefruit-tinged take on the Aviation, a Negroni Nuevo with the addition of hand-pressed orange, which I later found is the same as Dale DeGroff's Old Flame, and many other classic twists), the "Poolside Delights" (your basic poolside crowd pleasers with an eye on quality and presentation), and, finally, four "Extraordinary Mocktails."

Many may disagree with me here, but I find the inclusion of well thought out non-alcoholic cocktails to be not only an entirely easy way to generate additional revenue but also a fantastic test of the mixologist's ability to play with and meld flavors. Without the benefit of an alcoholic foundation, it is much harder to create a perfectly balanced and richly flavored drink. One of my training techniques has been to have bartenders create a non-alchoholic cocktail that attempts to rival that flavor and texture of a proper potable beverage. This test really grabs their attention and begins to help them understand the importance of proportion, temperature, texture, acidity, nose, and flavor layering. It is also worth mentioning that the inclusion of these Mocktail options is also, generally, greatly appreciated by our clients.

Of course, all of the drinks call for quality spirits and, more importantly, fresh ingredients. Getting the volume of fresh fruit, not to mention fresh herbs, has been quite a struggle. It can be done, and, more importantly, these cocktails can be executed consistently even in such a huge format.

CREATING THE FOUNDATION: THE KEYSTONE IN THE LONGEVITY OF ANY COCKTAIL PROGRAM

Welcome aboard!

After settling in to my closet, errr, cabin, I immediately meet with the Food and Beverage Management team to ensure all my materials and products have made it aboard (briefings, product lists, manuals, ingredients, etc.). When developing any beverage program, I recommend providing necessary materials and product lists at least 2-3 weeks before arrival to ensure you don't lose any valuable training days. There is nothing worse than arriving to discover an incomplete product list, a less than full roster of bartenders to train, and unprinted training materials. The Food and Beverage Manager and I then establish a mutually agreeable training schedule and a system of motivational procedures—disciplinary actions—for those who fall out of the loop. We are on a tight timeline, and there is little room for tomfoolery.

It is also at this point in the program where I am introduced to the head bartender. When this program began, the head bartender position didn't yet exist. The establishment of this figure is something I am proud to have been a part of. Now this is no ordinary head bartender position, the responsibilities and qualifications run more toward a highly experienced bar manager (i.e. strong business background)

with many years of bartending experience to boot. Having
someone whose sole focus is to ensure the program main-
tains the established standards is an irreplaceable piece
of any focused cocktail concept. The head bartender is
expected to take ownership of the program to maintain
consistency, and to train all new bar staff. This person can
conduct spirits seminars, cocktail classes for the guests,
and ensure the proper set-up of numerous daily events and
parties around the ship. As a consultant, it is my highest
recommendation that, regardless of the size of the operation, this position must exist in some form, or be created,
to make certain the original vision of the program is being
followed and fulfilled.

My first encounter with the bar staff is probably the
most important single hour I will spend on the ship. This
encounter can determine the success or failure of my mission.
It is at this crucial step where the "fire" is lit. Creating this
strong foundation in the bar staff begins by giving them a
deep understanding of the history of the craft, which will,
in turn, instill in them some pride in their profession, and
greater confidence to convey our service vision to the guests.
Believe it or not, most bartenders I encounter haven't been
exposed to the rich history of the cocktail and its rightful
place in the world of the culinary arts.

At the start of every new project, I do my best to take
the staff on a detailed journey through cocktail history, carefully noting dates and reflecting on important moments in
the development of our craft—the defining of the cocktail
in 1806, Jerry Thomas and his contributions, the story of
the martini, the golden years and the exceptional cocktail
craftsmanship leading up to Prohibition, Prohibition itself,
and, finally, bringing it all together to understand where
we are today (which is really not that far from where it
was 150 years ago). This is really where the passion and

the drive to excel are born. Gaining the trust and interest of the staff at this moment is paramount to leaving each ship with the envisioned result. More often than not in our industry, passion and success go hand in hand. They say knowledge is power. A bartender with a deep understanding and love for his craft is a powerful thing (from a financial perspective), and a wonderful sight to behold (from an artistic standpoint).

Working aboard a cruise ship demands a very fast learning curve. I find, more often than not, that I wind up running on high adrenaline while working to install these programs. The ship environment is far more fast-paced than the norm, and it takes a little while to figure out how to get the job done in the allotted time frame. My organizational skills have benefited greatly from this project, to say the least. One might find themselves becoming a Jedi of improvisation after a few weeks at sea.

I realized, almost immediately, that if I limited this crucial training session simply to giving a little history lesson to the bar staff, maybe demonstrating some new cocktail recipes, and then heading home, failure would be inevitable. You can't build a mansion on sand, nor can you install a successful cocktail program aboard a cruise ship without taking the proper steps to ensure it is built to last.

Creating systems of accountability may be the most important step to establishing the success of any bar program, especially those that float and deal with up to 2,000 drinkers, seven days a week, 365 days a year. With HAL, creating accountability begins with bartenders themselves—a change I had to make right away. Transferring more ownership of the bar from management to the guys working the bars was a big step to making sure that their execution remained consistent, while also, instilling in them a sense of pride in their work. Essentially, I believe

a bartender should manage his own bar, with supervisors
and bar management providing the necessary support, not
the other way around.

The consistent and complete use of checklists has
been our most important tool in getting the accountability
machinery rumbling. No less than 90 percent of the bars
I come across have either no working checklist or, if they
do have one, it has long since been kicked under the beer
cooler in favor of an easier open and close routine. I know
this because, year ago, I was the undisciplined kid doing this
at the bar. These checklists remain a living document that
must be constantly updated. A proper checklist thoroughly
encompasses all preparatory, operational, and breakdown/
cleaning procedures and expectations. Yet this checklist
is also much, much more. When executed correctly, it is
also a failsafe communication device.

Any issues that occur in a bar—low stock, maintenance
issues, etc.—are noted in detail, daily. The more detail,
the higher the likelihood of success. The checklist is then
double checked by both Head Bartender and also Beverage Director each day. As long as all items are noted, the
checklists are meticulously followed, and the bartender has
"managed" his/her bar, then the responsibility to follow
through with the requests is now squarely on the shoulders
of the management. So in this way, we create what I believe
to be an ideal support system. Everyone is doing what they
are supposed to be doing.

To go one step further, all checklists are collected at the
end of the night and turned into the Food and Beverage
Manager to be checked first thing the following morning.
The F & B (as we refer to him) checks this and follows up
with the head bartender and bar manager. Now, some of
you may think all this a little extreme, but the results of
this kind of detailed accountability have improved morale.

This process also undoubtedly helped to improve revenue generation through tighter reins on inventory and a far more streamlined bar set-up.

Each checklist works in tandem with a Product and Garnish Bar worksheet that is tailored to each bar. When opening the bar, the bartender preps exactly according to specifications and checks off on the checklist once it has been done. In addition to identifying proper preparation and closing procedures, each bar line tests different cocktails every single day. This happens in kitchens around the world, so why not in a bar? If your bar uses a fresh sour mix made each day, it is imperative to taste not only the batch but also the individual containers to be sure the mix transferred correctly. I have had many problems with this in the past.

While ensuring these levels of accountability are being implemented properly, I simultaneously begin a rigorous bar training and motivational process. This training not only includes the new signature cocktails, but also classic cocktail preparations, spirits knowledge, and also some sales techniques.

TRAINING

Training always begins on each ship with a walk-through of the opening preparation to make sure we are ready to begin an uninterrupted session. The bar is set up to specifications as a normal bar would be—raining is far more successful when no short cuts are taken. We then run through some key classic cocktails—Martinis, Manhattans, Sours, Collinses, Sidecars, and several others—while emphasizing an understanding of flavor and balance. Each bartender makes the drink while reciting the recipe, crafting and serving the drink in front of me as if I were a passenger. No detail is overlooked during these sessions; we go so far as to have them place each napkin in a certain direction (logo facing the guest every time), and always have them place the garnish at two o'clock using steel tongs, of course. Lounge servers are also present so they too can feel a certain sense of ownership in the program. For smaller clients, it has been my practice to train both bartenders and servers exactly the same way, so that everyone can make drinks with fantastic results.

The focus here is on proper technical execution and, once again, with an emphasis on the principle that crafting fine drinks really lies in the smallest details. It is important to impress upon the staff that shaking a drink too little or too much, which we have standard timings on, will greatly affect the quality of the cocktail, and that a stirring spoon is sometimes just the right tool to make the sublime old school cocktail.

There is also a mandate that jiggers must be used at all times, as this is the only way to truly keep the drinks consistent and the costs inline. I even have them jigger the fresh juices and sweetening agents, which, I can only imagine, will make many of you gasp. I have long wondered how far we can go to ensure a consistent cocktail, and this step has helped me get closer. My concern, though, is not so much in the pour of the base spirit (pouring 1.5 ounce and 2 ounce proportions can be easily taught), but in the pour of the mixers. It is here where missing even a 0.25-ounce measure can throw everything off.

This method is an extreme step and takes time to perfect. I can, however, cite several examples in London and New York where I see bartenders successfully applying jiggers to all signature cocktails (Dylan Prime, Milk and Honey, and the Pegu Club, to name a few). As we all know, a little goes a long way, and many bartenders tend to lean on mixers to add volume to their cocktails, bringing it up higher in the glass. Along this line of thought, I am also a huge proponent of smaller cocktail glasses (but that's for another time).

We then move into making the signature drinks following the same format. I break the bartenders into smaller training groups to make sure I have their full attention and because, well, the ship never sleeps and someone has to be in the Ocean Bar to fix Stingers for a group of older gentleman watching the waves, and younger women, roll by.

Testing occurs daily and I find these guys learn faster moving swiftly through smaller bunches of material as opposed to one obnoxious test at the end on sixty signature cocktails plus classics (which I give them anyway.) Tests are scored and are part of a certification process that includes attaining a minimum written test score and detailed personal skills evaluation.

UNLEASHING THE NEW PROGRAM ON THE UNSUSPECTING CRUISER: FINE TUNING THE EXECUTION

Once we are satisfied (or running out of time) with the training, preparations are made to install the new cocktail menus ship-wide. This can be a frustrating task. On more than one occasion, I have found myself having to walk the ship, bow to stern, just to make sure the pages are in the right order, and that the correctly formatted menus are in the correct bars.

Speaking of menus, without question a well thought out menu is an irreplaceable tool in moving drinks. While there are several approaches to writing a menu, I am a firm believer in painting a "flavor portrait" with each description. On the ship, guests have time to peruse a cocktail menu, and will usually do so rather thoroughly. Once again, it is a kitchen mentality that grabs me, so I find myself focus-

ing on creating value based on the complete cocktail and
craftsmanship, and not only on the spirit being used. I find,
more often than not, that guests really enjoy opening the
cocktail menu and reading vivid and sometimes educational
descriptions where they can almost taste the cocktail before
it actually gets to the table. This style is concept specific,
and so maybe isn't right for a nightclub, but it works bril-
liantly for a cruise lines, and for fine dining atmospheres
where people are in search of an experience.

So the menus are out and the drinks start flying. The
signature Mojitos, a drink I find bartenders have a love/
hate thing going on with all over the world, are causing
ships to run through up to 50 pounds of mint a week on
Caribbean itineraries. Have you ever seen a 50-pound
bag of mint???... Words just cannot do it justice. While
for the Alaska cruises, Espresso Martinis move like hot
cakes. Understanding the importance of the ever-changing
environment a cruise ship operates in is very important.
While on land, chefs and bartenders can change the menus
seasonally, but on a cruise ship climates and surroundings
can change on a dime. Training puts a strong emphasis on
these quick changes, and cocktails are adjusted accordingly
to maximize sales. Spanish Coffees may work as you putt
around Glacier Bay, for example, but not when anchored
off the shores of Trinidad, where a Daiquiri is indispensable—extra bitters for me, please.

As each implementation comes to an end, the focus
begins to return to the established operational standards,
making sure the accountability we worked so hard to create
is firing on all cylinders. I will walk the ship several times a
day with the management team until I am confident they
are seeing the important details that make the program
what it is. This time spent with managers is also designed
to once again establish pride in the product and build an

awareness of how great a cocktail experience can really be. I really want them to own this thing, as it were.

I will also be mindful of promotional aspects of the program and work with the cruise director to make sure it is promoted during ship activities, in the daily program, and during sail away events. Featuring appropriately selected cocktails at the first sail away of the cruise has an enormous impact on what the cruisers will be drinking for the next seven days.

As I write, I have implemented the program on nine of the fourteen ships and look forward to an opportunity to complete the job in 2006. It is an experience that continues to grow smoother and more rewarding as it goes along. The greatest perk of being a consultant is the satisfaction of seeing dramatic positive changes happen so swiftly in both the product and in the staff's understanding of the craft. Moving from one ship to the next, or one project to the next, can be extremely tiring, but the revitalization that comes with each success makes the whole thing worth it ten times over.

Well, just about the best thing for me about being on ship is the gentle rolling of the ocean. I find this gives me an amazingly peacefully slumber (everyone should experience this at least once). I need it too; I only ever seem to have enough time for five or six hours of sleep a day when I am at sea.

Will this program live up to expectations? Only time will tell, and many challenges still need to be overcome; but it is certainly moving in the right direction. This opportunity has certainly helped me define my own personal approach to my profession and I hope those in a similar facility will be able to pull something from this, as well. I am now convinced with a little more passion, and attention to detail in the areas of organization, proper training, and accountability, we can begin to see excellent cocktails and unforgettable bar experiences, not only at today's modern speakeasies, but at larger and more unexpected venues as well.

THE WORLDWIDE COCKTAIL CLUB

CONVERSATIONS WITH
HENRY BESANT AND DRÉ MASSO

BY JARED BROWN AND ANISTATIA MILLER

For the past fourteen years, British bartenders have given the Yankees a run for their money when it comes to striving for professionalism in the industry and forming a community to share knowledge. Jared Brown and Anistatia Miller sat with two of London's finest talents to discuss the future of the cocktail from a British perspective and the need for the profession to think global.

FORMED IN AUGUST 2004, the Worldwide Cocktail Club is a global cocktail community formed by top London mixologists Henry Besant and André ("Dré") Masso, who are striving to raise the bar by mobilizing a body of talent in related disciplines around in the world and disseminating the group's knowledge of bar operations, brand development, cocktail program creation, training, and event planning to the beverage industry at large.

We sat down with Henry and Dré at The Lonsdale in London's Notting Hill neighborhood to discuss their views on the current state of the beverage industry over outrageously good Hedgerow Slings and Fancy Bourbon Cocktails.

Anistatia Miller: What got you started?

Henry Besant: For me, personally, I always wanted to be a bartender, an actor, or a footballer—one of the three. Bartending was the thing I ended up doing. When I got started, it was a time in London when the industry was quite a dark place. Cocktails were only consumed in hotel bars, which maintained the high levels of standards and sophistication: places like the Savoy, Claridge's and more recently The Lanesborough. But outside of that there was nothing really going on. It was the age of TGI Friday's, here. That was the only place where people were really drinking cocktails.

I was always interested in cocktails. I read a lot. I was very fortunate when I first started. In the UK, you can't be a bartender until you're eighteen. I started washing glasses behind the bar when I was sixteen. I was fascinated by the experience of bars and particularly of cocktails. Totally by chance, I ended up working in a bar in Chelsea with a bartender called Dick Bradsell.[99] He sparked my imagination. Dome was a restaurant/bar/brasserie that was serving cocktails. I was inspired by that experience. Dick went on to create some of the modern classics we know internationally today.

I started to view bartending as a profession. I worked here in west London, in a place called Mas Café in Notting Hill for four years. I was a big proponent of cocktails and had a large cocktail list. The industry basically started at that time. For the first time, brand companies in London started to say "why don't you try this product because it's better" rather than because it's cheaper. They started to have things like comparative tastings and hold competitions among bartenders. A kind of community started to form. This was fourteen years ago in London.

People started to get to know each other. People started to know what I was doing over here and what somebody was doing in Soho, what somebody was doing somewhere else. A couple of years later, in 1994, a place called Atlantic opened, which was really a grand venue that focused on the cocktail.[100] Dick had his eponymous Dick's Bar there. That really fast-tracked the London industry. I found myself forgetting about football and acting and getting straight in there. I sadly bartend very infrequently now, but I bartended for about 10 years—five days, six days a week. Then as you do in the UK, I naturally graduated into a bar management position and have been fortunate to work in and help set up some very exciting and well-received bars in London.[101]

---

99. One of the legends of the London bar scene since the 1980s, Dick Bradsell created drinks like the Vodka Espresso, Gin Bramble, and Detroit Martini at Groucho's, The Zanzibar Club, Atlantic Bar, Café de Paris, and Pharmacy.

100. Some of the earliest cocktail competitions for Henry's generation of bartenders were held there.

101. Besant was director and general manger of 57 Jermyn Street; oversaw bar operations for the St Martin's Lane and Sanderson Hotels; and oversaw the Trafalgar Hotel's Rockwell bar and restaurant. He is the director of The Lonsdale and with partner Dré Masso has opened Green and Red plus, The All-Star Lanes.

AM: What were you doing, Dré?

Dré Masso: My trail was kind of similar. I'm a Londoner and my family is from Colombia. I guess my earliest memories are with my mother, a single parent who worked in bars and restaurants and who often took me to those places. My first memories are of playing with chefs, bartenders, and waitresses (waitresses were the best bit).

Collecting glasses, working bars, restaurants, clubs, doing what I felt really familiar with—that's what I did. I studied photography but that's [an] expensive hobby and profession to take forward. To pay for the chemicals and the equipment, it was natural to work in bars and get an extra bit of cash.

I guess at the time, it became more of a profession, something I could see myself doing for years. Actually, having a goal to make it something really special for myself did it. I guess all my friends were off to university doing their thing, I said to myself 'they're off for three years, let me see where I can get in three years.'

I worked my way up at the Atlantic,[102] which sadly closed this year. It was a big eye-opener for me. There was an amazing legend there, a Brazilian guy called Gavin Chase, who had certain way of doing things. He was a perfectionist and was very good at giving off that passion to other people.

So he really started opening me to the cocktail and good quality drinks. (Before that I hadn't really had a good experience with drinks.) He had very good classic cocktail training. That's where it started. Since then, I've been lucky enough to work at the LAB, which has been institution on the London bar scene—kind of a blueprint for today's cocktail environment. People have been there or studied the bartenders or the drinks. Now you can see any of those drinks in any bar in London.

102. Besides the Atlantic Bar, Dré worked at Salvador & Amanda, LAB, 10 Room, Tokyo Joe's, and The Londsale.

I also worked with Jamie Oliver, at the chef's [Fifteen] restaurant, which was very inspirational, because you are working with the chefs very closely. Downstairs there, they have a bar connected to the kitchen. You see these amazing chefs experimenting with things. Those guys influenced me in terms of flavors and putting things together.

I love traveling. I have traveled at lot. It was after my travels in the States that I got together with Henry and realized that we were both at a similar level.

Henry's very modest. His specialty skills are within management. I heard about these skills and I said, "Look. I like bartending and heard you're great at management. Can we do that together?"

So we did that here at The Lonsdale. At the same time, we were both receiving calls about putting a list together, or training some people, or doing some brand development. It was at that time we realized it would be stupid not to do this....

AM: ...to do an evolution and take it...

DM: ...take it more seriously and make some money from it and help each other.

AM: In other words, actually make money from drinking for a living. So the Worldwide Cocktail Club, what is it and why?

DM: I personally always love the word "club," because it hopefully involves everyone. There's something lovely about the Buena Vista Social Club.[103] It just sounds really appealing to the masses, I think. Originally, because we're based in London, we considered calling it the London Cocktail Club. And then maybe go and do the Barcelona Cocktail, then have these different clubs or companies or branches.

---

103. The title of an award-winning documentary by Wim Wenders and Ry Cooder, featuring the music of the Cuban Ensemble.

For whatever reason, we wanted to go global, to involve cocktail communities around the world, and put them into one melting pot. The Worldwide Cocktail Club was born. Our focus is anything drink related. Henry's fifteen years of experience and my twelve years experience, it's close to thirty years of collective knowledge we can use to help people.

Then there's the writing thing. We recently had our first book published, *Margaritas Rocks,* and we contribute to *Theme* magazine.

HB: The ethos for The Worldwide Cocktail Club was the club element, trying to unite the different cocktail cultures. It is a very grand idea, it always was, and still is. We're very basic people really. It may well not come to anything. But the momentum it has gathered over the last eighteen months has been extraordinary. It shows most of all that people are keen to reach out to each other internationally and progress the industry as a whole.

All we will ever try to do is to remain as independent but as supportive of everything within the industry as possible as long as it is respectful of its roots, respectful of its history, and of quality. An idea can be as off the wall as it might be or as modern as it would like to be. As long as those basic principles are in place then we're all for it. The difficult bit for us is that we really haven't worked out what it is in its true identity.

DM: How do we join? Where's our membership card?

HB: Can you send me an application form? How much do we pay? We literally get four emails a day, asking how much is the registration fee?

At this stage, it's not what it's about. We want, if anything, to create something that perhaps could branch over into a consumer market: where people could go to a sort of central focal point to learn about drinks or cocktails.

Quickly after we started, we wrote a manifesto for the company. We started talking to a few friends of ours in the industry.

We ended up getting picked up to work with Pernod-Ricard on a cocktail experience. We were allowed to create a program of all-encompassing 2-day, 3-day, or 4-day experiences. In this case, it happened to be branded by Wyborowa Vodka. It's different from a [typical] salesperson coming in waving a t-shirt saying "this is the only vodka that's worth tasting" or "try this in a Martini it knocks the socks off of every other vodka".

Thankfully these guys were forward thinking. We spent a lot of time and put a lot of effort into creating this program. We've been lucky to be management for the past ten years and learn that brand programs are all brand oriented. There wasn't anybody coming to you saying, "We can help you, support you, develop you, improve your skills. We can teach you about Pete Petoit and the Bloody Mary and Harry MacElhone. We can teach you about the Martinez Cocktail, teach about Mesopotamia and the origins of alcohol, and we can teach about all these things all in one go. We can give you a really good time and take you out in the city. We can even make a community within your own city."

One of the things that's really driven London is the fact that there was a community founded. It's the community that's really driven things forward more than anything else. Trade magazines have been important. Consumer interest has been important. The thing that has really been driving it has been a joint ethos of wanting to be good and wanting to be better. That's what provided the experience for wanting to do a global thing.

AM: What it seems like you're trying to do is accelerate what happened over the past 200 years into less than a decade: when the cocktail went from America to Europe to

places like Singapore and Rangoon and to Hong Kong when
the Royal Navy took gin and rum around the world.

HB: It's only doing what's been done before. But because
the world is a much smaller place it's more feasible to do.

DM: We often say that your city [New York] has a
bar scene very similar to the London bar scene about
fourteen years ago, distilling all that information all that
experience.

HB: We always say that when people say, "Oh, it'll
never catch on. We say, "Okay, we'll show you evidence
that it does catch on." And then people travel and they
do see. When they have a Manhattan in London or in
New York they want the same experience when they go
to Zurich or Romania.

AM: The joy of jet age travel. Look at how many of
us have traveled; especially those of us from London and
from New York, it is easy access. It's easy to say, "Okay, I'm
going to spend a weekend in Rome or spend a weekend in
Barcelona." And you're discovering ingredients, discovering
things you never knew about. When we went to Florence
and Turin last year, we discovered the aperitivo. Here's
something that's a 150 years old and people in the US are
just discovering it.

HB: Like we were discussing before, when you were
introducing people in Oslo to the Vodka Espresso. They
got the espresso machine in the middle the bar. They've
got the vodka. It's all there. They just need some kind of
guidance.

Another classic example was when we were in Romania. We discovered watermelons grow in abundance there.
This was a kind of ground zero starting point that's changed
things since we've been there. Last time we visited, there
were loads of people making Espresso Martinis and Fresh
Watermelon Martinis as a result of our visits. It was a very
rewarding experience.

DM: They were making cocktails before that. They had ten ingredients. Five of those ingredients were syrups and sugars.

HB: They weren't using the right ones, really.

AM: Sounds like we're starting a slow-food movement.

JB: But we are.

AM: Yes we are. Now as The Worldwide Cocktail Club, on the eve of the cocktail's bicentennial, where do you see the future of the cocktail?

JB: Will we continue to call it a cocktail or will we call it a Martini?

AM: Or will we call it a drink?

JB: The cocktail was a fairly well defined concept in its day. And now anything even a glass of wine can be a cocktail in its broadest sense.

HB: Standing back from it, I see the word "cocktail" as a very good generic term for mixed drinks, while recognizing its spirits-sugar-water-bitters origin, listening to, dismissing, and agreeing with various arguments along the way about what classifies a cocktail. I think, if you look at the various potential origins of the word cocktail the basic mixed nature of it. Our favorite is in H.L. Mencken's *American Language*, where he talks cocktail being the shortened form of "cock tailings," the name of a mixture of tailings from the barrels of various liquors thrown together in a common receptacle and sold at a low price in a tavern.

AM: That's so romantic.

HB: Kind of skuzzy. The mixed nature of the word "cocktail," to me, is something that makes it quite a generic definition of mixed drinks. I think in terms of the future of the cocktail, I think there's a hell of a long way to go. I think the word "cocktail" is a very useful moniker for a mixed drink. I think it's something that should be embraced, especially now that it's 200 years old, and should be given credence. I think the cocktail has been very resilient over the years since then, and lasted in various different countries, and during various dark times, should it be Prohibition or financial poverty.

JB: ...or the seventies.

HB: ...or the seventies. And it's still there and it's still referred to. And I personally think it's here to stay. It's a good word and a good definition.

DM: I love the word itself. It oozes fun and good times and occasion. It sounds good and looks good. It is a globally recognized word.

HB: We were talking about this earlier. The consumer jump is the big one to focus on. I see the industry almost going around full circle on itself, almost speaking up its own ass, and getting far too fanciful—beyond its age and maturity. It's not at a stage where you can go even in London or New York—two of the world's most recognized cocktail experience cities—and find more than five or six bars, maybe less, that you can be sure you can get a good drink in. That's the reality of it.

What's wonderful is that there are so many bars that are trying. It's not snobbery. I love it. It's a passion. I want it to be good. I want it to be a good cocktail experience if you're in a neighborhood in south London or east London or wherever.

AM: Do you think the evolution of the cocktail is happening the same way food happened in the past 25 years? Before then, our view of food in London and New York was edible plonk[104] and then people discovered things. You could have salmon madras and tikka whatever. You could have anything in the world because people were experimenting so hard with new ideas and pushing it—so hard they forgot about the essentials. They forgot about the mathematics of

---

104. Cheap or inferior wine.

food. They forgot to go back to the basics before evolving. Do you think it's at that same point?

HB: Yes it is. For example in the UK, specifically London, the city has wonderful quality and definition of quality within all its different styles of cuisine. The quality is incredible. But it is only in the last ten years that it's happened. But prior to that, with food, it took many, many more years. Cocktails are on a parallel path. It's just happened in London. There are highly skilled people in many regions. There are some very, very good bars in Newcastle, in Edinburgh, in Oxford...

DM:...in Brighton...

HB: ...and this is something that is very different: That you can get quality across the country. The signs are all positive. But we need to be very wary of extending ourselves as an industry before getting the basics right.

JB: The basics. You've got someone who comes to you and says, "I'm opening a bar." What would your basic advice be?

HB: My number one rule is do what you do; small or large just do what you do. Do it very well.

DM: Keep it simple. People try too hard to be too extravagant and then disappoint. Like the ingredients you're using in drinks, a lot of time less is more.

JB: That's what's missed by a lot of the people who start into the cocktails and want to really impress.

AM: So how much do you want to espouse to aspiring professional bartenders that there's more to life than creating cocktails. How much attention do you pay to your customer and to the business?

DM: One of the best people in the business who writes about this is Gary Regan. He really talks about what a bartender is. It's really important.

AM: Gary comes of the 1970s generation that served Sex on the Beach, the Long Island Iced Tea, and the

Harvey Wallbanger. But it was the ambience he created
around his bar.[105]

DM: I never experienced it, but you get the feeling he could control the room.

AM: He did and does.

DM: And have that air of power, and make sure it's tame when it needs to be tame, and lively when it needs to be lively.

JB: You're touching very subtly on one of his methods of control, which is controlling the music. He will change the music to shift the mood in the room. He'll interrupt conversations when he hears them going sour. And he'll spike them in the right direction.

AM: But you have to when you're creating an experience. It's not just the cocktails. It's the entire experience.

HB: It's like the old adage: If someone wants to drink alone: stay at home, get out the blended scotch whiskey, and drink it down in one. You go out to a bar to go out to a bar, to interact, to have an experience—the experience of drinking, the experience of being in a creative environment. Maybe you get laid. Maybe you do something bad, maybe you don't. Maybe you socialize with somebody you haven't seen in a while. Whatever it is it's an experience other than the drink.

AM: That's the UK experience. There was an old couple in the place where I grew up who every week, on Tuesday, would come into the pub and bring a board game with them. The wife always had a glass of wine, while the husband had a pint. The rest of the town came in to say hi to them while they played Pachisi.

HB: In a way, once you know how to create a pleasant environment, it doesn't have to be high design or high spec, just a pleasant environment. I think the quality of-

---

105. Drake's Drum in New York.

drinks—even the most basic of spirits and mixed drinks—the standards are still not high enough.

In terms of the bartender experience—to be greeted correctly, asked what you'd like to drink in the right manner, to have a certain level of knowledge about what you're serving, and a certain level of care in the way that it's served, the cleanliness of the glassware, amount of ice, freshness of the mixer—I'd like to think that probably beyond all of our lifetimes, we could go into the most basic of places that purport to be a bar and get that kind of care.

In a pub, you're not getting the care for a gin and tonic like you do an ale: generally, it's served in a small wine goblet with a small cube of ice—or no ice—and a moldy strip of lime.

JB: In a certain warm-weather city in the US that I won't mention, where they make some of the best cocktails in the US, a bartender opens the garnish tray, which is refreshed once a week, and adds a citrus compost slice to your drink.

HB: I'm really excited about the changes I've seen in my lifetime within the industry and the rebirth—the renaissance—of the cocktail. But also I'm mindful of the fact that's it's only at this stage in a niche market and that's the fence we try to jump over in whatever small way we can.

JB: Is that because of supply, demand, or both?

HB: I think its more demand-oriented.

JB: So you have an opportunity to walk into an auditorium filled with young drinkers, who are just coming of age, you step up to the podium and what do you whisper, say, or scream at them?

HB: In an auditorium full of virgin drinkers, I say something like "Margaritas" and I make them really well-made Margaritas—give them a real understanding.

AM: ...and then make them real Mai Tais.

HB: It's kind of like I mentioned before, this is the next big thing—people understanding what they're ordering. People understand what music they like and what clothes they like, how they want their hair cut. They're really understanding what food they like—now. The consumers are getting more focused on themselves and what they like and what they want.

In the US although, it's very marketing led. People do brand call. They do cocktail call. But they tend not to know if they're good or bad when they get them. That's my impression. The drinks they brand call are advertising or media driven, celebrity driven. I think a massive step up would be if consumers knew more about what they're consuming, in terms of drinks.

AM: So ultimately, we need to convince people that individuality is the best way to select a cocktail.

JB: Same question to you, Dré.

DM: I think everybody's got to be individual. Try things. Be experimental. Try them again. Be experimental again. I think you have to try things two or three or four times before you really get it. Don't necessarily believe the hype that surrounds drinks. You need to acquire a taste for things. Trust the barman. Communicate with your bartender.

THE NITTY GRITTY

*The one thing we realized when we
published the first Mixologist:*
The Journal of the American Cocktail
*is how many people are fascinated by the
minute details of cocktail creation—the variations of the composition of simple syrup,
the attention to detail in the construction
of a* Martini. *In this edition, two main
components of a number of libations are
the subjects of consideration. Ice—the back-
bone of any cocktail—and sour mix are this
edition's reflections, guaranteed to make
you think twice and thrice about what goes
into your drink.*

ICE-COLD THOUGHTS

BY AUDREY SAUNDERS

Ice is the one of the most important ingredients in a cocktail and one of the most ignored by bartenders. How it is made, what size should be used for a particular drink, and how to use it are Audrey Saunders obsessions as she presents her take on this hot subject.

SIZE DOES MATTER. And I should elaborate that we are talking about ice here. In a perfect world, you would be able to handcraft ice for each glass you stock, but that sort of preparation is unrealistic for a busy commercial bar operation producing in large volume. And frankly, not many people are going to carve out a block of ice with a pick for a large-volume bar. Yet ideally, there would be large cubed ice, cracked ice, and crushed ice, and this is definitely achievable.

You want large, full cubes when you are going to have something like a whiskey on the rocks, or a gin and tonic. The full-sized cube is a larger, denser mass. Precisely because of its larger size, it has a dramatically slower rate of melting. The larger the cube is, the slower it melts. And if you ask for something on the rocks, you want it to stay on the rocks, right? Otherwise you would have asked for a whiskey and water.

Most of the commercial ice machines currently on the market produce small ice chips, and much of the time these have hollow centers. If you pick up one of these chips and hold it in the palm of your hand, it immediately becomes watery, and will start to melt within seconds. When you fill a glass with these chips, their shape allows them to pack in tightly, densely—it is deceptive because a small shot of spirits will fill up that glass to the top. With this visual, most people think that they are getting a real value—"Wow, that bartender really knows how to pour them." Yet it is a warped perception, because within minutes the drink has become overly diluted. When you utilize a "good" (larger) ice cube, a shot of spirit will not fill the glass to the brim…but this larger, colder mass will take a lot longer to melt, which will prevent it from becoming watered down too quickly. The only downside to the shot poured over larger cubes is that it doesn't raise the drink-line to the top, so the uneducated consumer isn't able to visualize the benefits. But if producing great cocktails matters to you, then it's up to you to make the changes necessary. It is up to you to educate your guests and change their perception.

In all honesty, this simply boils down to what kind of operator you wish to be. If you are looking to crank out drinks without a care to quality, then by all means, carry on without a second thought. But if you truly do care about the quality of the product you're putting out there, then you should take your ice very seriously.

These commercial ice chips ruin cocktails. Because they dilute the drink so rapidly, you can't ever really achieve a cold drink temperature with them. For drink preparation, the bartender needs to measure ingredients into a glass, add ice, and shake well, right? You need to shake well to get it cold, but these small chips dissolve in the shaking process, and what you wind up with is an over-diluted drink. Think about how quickly even a non-alcoholic soda goes flat over this ice.

Okay, so now you're equipped with this information the next time you're out ordering a drink—maybe you'll ask the bartender not to shake it so long or hard, because you don't want it to be overly watery. Or maybe you won't simply because you don't want to be a pain in the ass. Consequently the drink you receive will be a little too warm and intense. Welcome to cocktail hell.

I've installed a Kold Draft machine in The Pegu Club. I chose it because this machine produces big, cold, beautiful ice cubes. I'm utilizing their largest ice mold, which produces a cube 1.25 x 1.25 x 1.25 inches. Sure, it takes more power on the bartender's part to shake with this bigger ice, but its well-worth it. Not only do you get lovely, delightfully icy-cold drinks with it, but selfishly, it's also enjoyable for me to watch my bartenders shaking like that. (Friends have told me the same.) I believe that the ability to shake these big ice cubes for a full shift truly separates the men from the boys.

And people say that the liquor industry is a real boys' club.

But back to ice again. Cracked ice has more exposed "surface area," and will emit more coldness. The temperature of ice does vary, and ideally you would prepare cracked ice only as you need it. Freshly cracked ice will produce a very cold Martini, which is, of course, optimal. Imagine taking a full cube and giving it a thwack to break it up—it is at that very point when cracked ice is at its coldest. Yet you need to use it ASAP—as it sits out, the atmospheric temperature will set in and raise the temperature of the ice, reducing the coldness.

Also think about why a Martini made with frozen ingredients (i.e. spirits kept in the freezer) is never as good as one that is stirred over ice. The minute the "frozen" Martini warms up, it becomes hot and alcoholic and unpalatable, because it wasn't ever diluted in the first place.

Different Sizes and Shapes

I have a couple of Japanese silicone ice molds that are designed specifically to make ice balls. They are very cool and certainly fun to play with, but I think they are almost too big. It's like having the big boulder in *Indiana Jones* rolling toward you when you try to drink from your glass; I'm afraid my tooth will get chipped. Yet a few of these balls would be the perfect cooling agent in a big bowl of punch.

I have also experimented with balloons to achieve different shapes. Think of the water balloons that you used to make when you were a kid; balloons work well because they have the ability to expand as the water freezes. There are also a lot of interestingly-shaped silicone baking molds that work well too.

SPECIFIC ICE FOR SPECIFIC DRINKS

Martinis and Manhattans should be prepared by stirring with freshly cracked ice. Classically, these are "stirred" drinks. In the recent past I've heard frequent calls for "shaken" Martinis and Manhattans, but I believe this is because today's little ice chips simply aren't cutting it. Stirring big cubes that have been freshly thwacked and shattered are the way to go. Stir a drink over this and you'll enjoy a delightfully silky experience (without the aeration from shaking). It's my personal theory that the phrase "bruising the gin" came from the over-dilution caused by utilizing crappy ice.

Crushed ice is ideal for drinks like the mint julep; if you add undiluted spirits into a drink, you will need the dilution you get from crushed ice. There is a category of drinks that are referred to as "mists;" simply a shot of spirit served directly into a glass of crushed ice. They are icy-cold, and refreshing in the very same way a frappe is, because of the combination of diluted spirit and ice. People who order mists are doing so precisely because they expect that combination of dilution and coldness.

But it is the very qualities of crushed ice that serve as a downfall in blender drinks. We love the coldness and the texture of the frozen drink, but its rapid dilution creates its own demise. It is this same reason why I've experimented with freezing various drink ingredients prior to adding them to the blender. In my mind, if I want a frozen daiquiri, why not freeze the lime juice and simple syrup prior to blend-

149

ing? This way, you are not going to over-dilute the drink by adding excess ice to frappe. Your ingredients will then serve as the "actual" ice, but also important to keep in mind, is that you cannot solely rely on frozen ingredients to complete the drink—you will still need to add a small amount of real ice for proper dilution (drinks should be diluted with approximately 20-25 percent water to help achieve balance). You don't want to use whole cubes directly in the blender as it can wear on the motor; neither would crushed ice work because it would dilute much too rapidly. Cracked ice is best here.

But we are a long way's away from perfecting the blender drink. These are just preliminary thoughts for the time-being.

Prettier Ice for the Home User

There are a few variables that can help here. Hard water has a lot of minerals in it, which contributes to cloudy ice. You want to use softened water, or even distilled water, as it has all the minerals removed. You can also boil the water prior to freezing it, as boiling will remove dissolved air—as ice freezes, dissolved air bubbles get trapped in the ice, contributing to cloudiness. Freezing warm water or lowering the temperature in your freezer will also help to slow down the rapidity at which the cube gets frozen—which will greatly aid in allowing those air bubbles to free themselves.

Perfectly clear ice is difficult to achieve at home, though. Commercial units have ice plates in which a continual flow of water is run. Envision a mini water fountain with enclosed walls—the streams of water are continually running over the inside of the walls. The walls are refrigerated plates, and as the water runs over them, they will slowly build up thin layers of ice. Icicles that we see formed on trees are crystal clear because snow water is pure and free of impurities. That pureness combined with tiny amounts of water droplets allows it to freeze in the thinnest of layers—which form a crystal clear formation.

I frequently get inquiries about "What's Hot," "Trends," or "What's the Next Big Thing." While I agree that it's important to forge ahead in that direction, we need to put even more emphasis on the basics of what is paramount to a well-made drink. Ice is a huge factor in this, and you don't have to be an artisan mixologist to make that change. Improving on your ice is something that everyone can do.

THE DEFINITIVE GUIDE TO SWEET & SOUR

BY DARCY S. O'NEIL

Thought you knew everything about making the essential sweet and sour mixer? Mixologist's favorite chemist returns with his study of sour mix, giving a few tips on citrus selection and a science experiement to perform on your own.

SWEET, SOUR, BITTER, AND SALTY— the four elements that make up taste sensations and the flavors that make a great drink. Of these, sweet and sour are the most important because they balance one another and make an enjoyable, thirst quenching drink.

There is no such thing as a perfect sour mix, but there is a perfectly balanced drink.

One of the best-known examples of a well-balanced sweet and sour drink is wine. Yes, a good wine is the perfect harmony of sweet and sour. In wine there are two predominant flavor characteristics and they are sweetness, the sugar content, and sourness, the acid content. Bitter and salty are minor characteristics. The terms astringency and spiciness, although commonly used to describe wines, are actually tactile sensations in wines, and not flavors. When sweet and sour are in balance, they make for a great drink. Even ice wine, with its high residual sugar levels, up to 20 percent, can be enjoyable if the grape has good acidity. In the wine world they like to use the term acid to refer to sour, it is a technically more accurate term, plus it makes for better marketing.

So, the key to understanding sourness in cocktails is to focus on the acids present in your drink. Now, what exactly are these acids and how do they compare in sourness? Well, there are many different types of acids in the fruit used to make wine or sour mix, but the essential ones for our purpose are citric acid, malic acid, tartaric acid, and ascorbic acid.

Citric Acid: This substance occurs naturally in most fruits and is the most popular single fruit acid in the food and beverage industry. It is simple to use and has a pleasant tangy flavor. Citric acid also has a vital function in human and animal metabolism. Indeed, the citric acid cycle is one of the body's most important metabolic pathways. Of the four acids here, citric is considered to present a fresh taste.

Malic Acid: The pleasant, refreshing experience of biting into a juicy apple or cherry is partly caused by malic acid. Malic acid has a clean, mellow, smooth, lingering tart taste. A key characteristic of this acid is that it enhances fruit flavors, masks the aftertaste of some salts, and provides ten to twenty-five percent more sourness than citric acid. Of the four acids here, malic acid has a "green apple" tartness.

Tartaric Acid: This is the predominant acid in grapes, which gives wine its characteristic taste. It is used as an acidulent in beverages, especially grape and lime flavored beverages. Tartaric acid has a sharp acid taste and can be considered the harshest of the four acids here.

Ascorbic Acid: Most commonly found in fruit, but it is higher in citrus fruits like lemons and limes, ascorbic acid is the chemical name for vitamin C. This acid is very unstable and will break down if heated. Citric acid has a sour taste similar to the flavor of a lime.

TESTING THE WINE THEORY

A good demonstration of the sweet and sour wine principle is to actually make a cocktail, using these components, that tastes like wine. To make this drink you will need the following items; naturally sweet white grape juice, pisco or grappa or vodka, and "acid blend" (a combination of 25 percent citric, 25 percent malic and 50 percent tartaric acid, which is available at your local wine making store). Acid blend is very cheap to purchase. Pure tartaric acid will also work in this cocktail. You may also want to add something, like white vermouth, gin, or brandy, to make the drink a little more complex.

The most important part of this drink is getting the acid blend correct. To do this you will need to dissolve 1 tablespoon (roughly 12 grams) of the acid blend powder into 1/2 cup (120 milliliter) of hot water. The tartaric acid may not dissolve completely, so the solution may look milky. Prior to adding it to your cocktail just shake the solution. Once it is added to your cocktail it will dissolve.

PLONK COCKTAIL
2 oz (60 ml) white grape juice
1.25 oz (35 ml) pisco / grappa / vodka
0.25 oz (7.5 ml) brandy / gin / vermouth (white)
0.5 oz (15 ml) acid blend solution
Shake with ice and strain into a wine glass.
Garnish with a lime wheel.

If you want to further adjust the cocktail to your liking, you can purchase each acid individually and add each in varying amounts. Just remember that tartaric acid is the main acid in wine. The quantity of sugar will depend on the type of grape juice you use.

This sweet/sour balance may be adjusted to taste. If the drink is too sweet, just add more acid blend solution, if the drink is too sour or tart simply add more grape juice.

For an even more authentic tasting Plonk Cocktail, purchase wine tannins from your winemaking supplier, and add them to your acid blend solution. Because you will need such a small quantity of tannins, your acid blend solution should be made in a greater volume. A general guideline is 1/8 teaspoon (0.5 grams) of tannins per 750 ml of acid blend solution. A more simple way to add tannins is to add half a teaspoon of strong steeped tea into the cocktail. Green tea gives a better cocktail color, but black tea will work just fine.

Alcohol content is also an important factor in getting the flavor of this cocktail right. Wine, and drinks in general, tolerate acidity better when the alcohol content is higher. A 5-ounce (150 ml) drink containing 1.5 ounce (45 ml) of 40 percent alcohol results in a drink with 12 percent alcohol, just like wine!

You may be surprised to find that, if done properly, this drink will actually taste just like wine, obviously not great wine, but better than some two day old house wines.

So now that we have a good background on the acidic ingredients used to create a sour flavor, and how they work. We need to look at our sources for these acids, and then how to balance these acids with sweetness in our cocktails.

Our Primary Acid Source

Not surprisingly, our primary sources for these acids are going to be lemons and limes. Since these fruits are rich in citric acid, have limited sugar content, and are relatively cheap, they are a perfect source.

About Lemons: There are 47 known varieties of lemons. The two basic types are: acid and sweet. The acid types are the ones we are interested in and, luckily, the most commercially available. The two most common types of sour lemons are the Eureka's and the Lisbon's. For marketing purposes, no distinction is made between the two varieties.

The Eureka lemon, sometimes referred to as the Four Seasons lemon, is probably the most widely grown lemon variety in the world. It is a true "bitter" lemon with a moderate amount of juice and acid content. This lemon has seeds and a thick skin.

Lisbon's are known for their bright yellow color, good texture, and higher juice content. This lemon is generally seedless which makes it useful for garnishes.

One medium lemon will product about 1.5 ounces (45 ml) of juice. Lemons have 1.4 grams of citric acid and 1 ounce (30 ml) ascorbic acid per 1 ounce (30 ml) serving. A lemon also has about 2.5 grams of sugar per 100 grams.

About Limes: The term "lime" refers to a distinct group of 160 citrus fruits. Limes are generally smaller and about 35 percent more acidic than lemons. The two most common types available are the Mexican lime (Key or Bartenders lime) and the Persian (Tahiti or Bearss lime). The higher citric acid levels give lime its mouth-watering sharp bite. This fruit has very low sugar levels of 0.5 grams per 100 grams.

Mexican Limes: This fruit is grown in Florida and Mexico, and is not always available throughout the year. This fruit is highly aromatic and more intensely flavorful than Persian-type limes. This type of limes contains seeds. Key limes can have an acid content of up to 8 percent or 2.4 grams per 1ounce (30 ml) serving.

Persian Limes: This fruit is larger and less flavorful than the Mexican lime. This lime is seedless and is useful for garnishes. Persian Limes have 1.8 grams of citric acid per 1 ounce (30 ml) serving.

In most recipes, lemon and lime juice are interchangeable. When substituting lime juice for lemon juice, the quantity of juice should be reduced by about a third. Depending on the quality and ripeness of your fruit, these numbers can vary, but in all likelihood this will not adversely affect the quality of your sour mix.

SECONDARY SOURCES OF ACID

Using fresh juice is highly recommended, as it will give your drinks excellent flavor. However, if fresh juice is not readily available or is deemed too expensive in certain seasons, in certain seasons, frozen or bottled juices will work. When using commercially produced juices you can substitute a portion of fresh squeezed juice, and the zest, to enhance the flavor. This provides a happy medium between cost and quality.

The other source for this acid is available from your local winemaking shop. The acids we used in the Plonk Cocktail can help make a quality sour mix that is both consistent and affordable. Just remember that the key acid in lemons and limes is citric acid.

Making a sour mix with just acids and flavoring is how most 'pre-mix' companies do it. It is not a recommended method for preparing sour mix, as it will lack the complex flavor oils of the lime/lemon fruit, and it will produce a "synthetic" taste in the final mix. These purified acids, however, can be used to balance and enhance flavors in your mix and drinks.

For the purist who feels that adding "chemicals" to a drink, such as citric and malic acid powder, is blasphemous, it should be noted that the wine industry "doctors" wines on a regular basis. Depending on the region, climate, or weather, many wines need a little help to reach their full potential. The addition of "additives", such as these acids, allows this to happen.

For example, in California, the warm climate causes the grapes to produce more sugar. In northern climates, like Canada, the grapes produce more acid. California law allows wineries to add acids to the grape juice (must) prior to fermentation, so as to balance out the final wine. If it's good enough for the wine industry, then it should be good enough for bartenders.

The key to a great sweet and sour drink is to make sure that there is a balance between the sugar and acidity. Neither flavor should overpower the drink, but they should definitely enhance the drink. A cocktail with too much sweetness will make the drink taste sugary, dull, and flabby. It will lack a vibrant refreshing quality. A cocktail with too much acid will taste harsh, sharp, and acidic; the flavors of the cocktail will be overridden by the sensation of acidity. If there is too much sugar and acid, as compared to the other flavor components, in your cocktails, your drink will taste like a sweet-tart. The sugar to acidity ratio in any given cocktail truly is a balancing act.

RECOMMENDATION

If possible, it is always best to use fresh ingredients, on a per drink basis, as needed. There are times when making each drink from scratch is not technically feasible, such as service bars and large parties. When time is at a premium, using a freshly made sour mix is the next best option.

SWEET & SOUR MIX

There really isn't a standard recipe for sweet and sour mix. Sour mix actually developed as a way for bartenders to improve efficiency, by preparing large quantities before a busy sales period. When improvements in efficiency enter the picture, it's almost always true that the quality of the final product will take a direct hit.

Over time, beverage companies decided to get into the market and create a very cheap, but consistent, industrial sour mix. This made it hard for bar owners to refuse, since fresh fruit and the labor involved in making a sour mix was expensive. However, this approach has lead to poor drink quality, so it is also recommended that you avoid these premixes.

For our purposes, we are going to look at two types of sour mix. Both of these are on the upper end of the quality spectrum. The first is the classic and easiest recipe, the citrus juice and sugar mixture. The second recipe will use a little chemistry to make a modern sour mix more acceptable to contemporary tastes. This recipe will also incorporate a few "tricks" to ensure final product consistency and to add beneficial characteristics to your cocktail—while staying true to the classic sour mix recipe.

THE CLASSIC SOUR MIX RECIPE

The original sour mix formula was just adding sugar, water and citrus juice directly into someone's drink:

I part lemon juice
I part simple syrup (2 sugars to I water)

The classic employment of sour mix is in the whisky sour. Back in the old days, most spirits were quite harsh, even for rough frontier workers. The idea was to soften the drink with sugar and lemon juice. The egg white gives the drink a smooth silky texture with a frothy head.

WHISKY SOUR
2 oz (60 ml) blended whisky
I oz (30 ml) lemon juice
I oz (30 ml) simple syrup (2:1)
dash egg white (optional)
Shake with ice and strain into a sour or rocks glass and garnish with orange and cherry.

By modern standards, this drink is considered to have rough edges. But back in the day, this was a smooth drink. A lot of the character of this drink is lost without the addition of the egg white.

Over the years people's tastes have changed. Specifically, there had been a trend in cocktails from strong to smooth. For example, a classic Margarita is too harsh for most people's palates. At most bars they make Margaritas as frozen drinks, which are much smoother and bare less resemble to the classic drink. But no one can argue with the sales volume of frozen Margaritas.

The classic sour mix is great for cocktail enthusiasts who want to be traditional. At most modern bars, however, the classic sour mix may be too bold or cloyingly sweet for customers who are looking for a smooth drink to relax and pass the time.

A Modern Sour Mix Recipe

This recipe is built upon the classic sour mix, but the goal is to create a mix that gives the cocktail a smooth texture, frothy head, good citrus flavor, and moderate sourness.

Before we get into the recipe, the number of ingredients may scare off a few traditionalists. Let me assure you that this recipe contains nothing more than sugar, citrus acids, and egg whites. The recipe simply calls for different ratios and different types of sugar and citrus acids.

SOUR MIX
1.5 cup (360 ml) sugar
0.5 cup (120 ml) corn syrup or glucose
0.5 cup (120 ml) maltodextrin
6 ounce (180 ml) fresh lemon juice
4 ounce (120 ml) fresh lime juice
2 tablespoons (30 ml) lime zest

2 teaspoons (8 gr) dehydrated egg white
1 teaspoon (4 gr) citric acid
2 cups (480 ml) water

Mix water, sugar, corn syrup (or glucose), maltodextrin, and lime zest in a pot and gently stir over heat until all the sugars have dissolved. Turn off the heat and add the remaining ingredients, stirring until dissolved. Strain the mix into a 750-ml bottle.

Maltodextrin is a simple sugar, like sucrose (table sugar) or fructose. It is made from two or more glucose molecules, and forms chains, similar to starch. Corn syrup or glucose is the simplest and most important sugar from a biological standpoint. Maltose (two glucose molecules bonded together) is about half as sweet as sucrose. Maltodextrin is commonly found in apricots, guava, and honey. It is used in baby foods and sports energy drinks as a source of carbohydrates. It acts as a viscosity modifier in liquids and a foam stabilizer in beer. In our sour mix it will help give a stable, frothy head and add smoothness and body to the cocktail. You will find that that there is a slight increase in the viscosity of the drink, which provides a silky sensation when drinking the cocktail. You can find this sugar at your local homebrew or winemaking store.

A good way to improve the citrus flavor of your sour mix is to add the zest from the peels and soak this in the mixture for ten minutes while you dissolve the sugars. The zest contributes a lot of flavor, from the oils in the skin. When grating the fruit, avoid using the white pith, as it is very bitter; grate the fruit first, before juicing. If you don't have time for this you can buy lemon and lime oils from higher end markets and culinary stores, but use these oils sparingly.

The additional ingredients, such as the citric acid, are used to make the drink more consistent, while the dehydrated egg whites provide extra body to the drink. Most establishments avoid using raw egg whites for health reasons, but if you can't find dehydrated egg whites you can usually find pasteurized eggs whites in your grocery store. Use two tablespoons of the liquid egg whites.

Another option for making your sour mix is to modify the types of acid. For example, you can add malic acid to give a different taste to your mix. Most commercial fruit beverages use a combination of malic and citric acids. Try a ratio of 30/70 citric acid to malic acid.

The final option is to use fructose in place of the sucrose. In lemons and limes, fructose is the naturally occurring sugars, along with glucose. Just remember that when substituting fructose, it is roughly twice as sweet as sucrose. If you can't find fructose at your local health food store, just put your regular table sugar into water, add a teaspoon of citric acid, and boil for five minutes. This will invert your sugar, which results in a solution of sucrose, fructose, and glucose.

If you compare the Whisky Sour recipe using the classic sour mix with the modern mix, you will notice a couple of things. First, the modern mix isn't as sweet as the classic version. This is because we are using two sugars that are not as sweet as pure sucrose. The classic Whisky Sour can be cloyingly sweet which makes the drink flat and flabby. The sweetness is out of balance with the rest of the ingredients.

The modern version is a little more balanced. You get the sour taste, which passes quickly and leads to a semi-sweet finish with little or no aftertaste. It also preserves the character of the base spirit by not being overly sweet or sour.

Whisky made today is also very different than the original distilled spirit. Most modern distillers are trying to make a smooth product that will appeal to a wide range of clients. When today's spirits are used in an old recipe, the balance may no longer work.

JUICING TIPS

1. Invest in a good quality hand juicer or press type juicer.
2. Room-temperature fruit will yield more juice than those that are refrigerated.
3. Use your palm to roll the lemons or limes around on the countertop a few times before squeezing.

CONCLUSION

When making a sour mix your options are almost endless. This doesn't mean, however, that your sour mix should be used in every cocktail that calls for sourness. Each cocktail should be prepared according to how the original creator wanted to express certain flavors. Using pre-made sour mix in a traditional margarita, for example, is probably a bad idea, but a drink like a Kamikaze or Amaretto Sour is a perfect opportunity to use your quality pre-made sour mix. With a good quality sour mix you can make some outstanding drinks that will impress customers and friends equally.

The recipes provided in this article are not the be-all-and-end-all of the sweet and sour spectrum; they are merely the beginning. Like all culinary pursuits, experimentation will only lead to great things.

SPIRITED HISTORY

We present for your consideration the liquor
that has stimulated the imagination like
none other in the history of spirits—
absinthe—as well as the story of rum, a true
workingman's spirit (which some people
also say changed the economy of the world)
and the story of the family that created the
world's most popular brand.

ABSINTHE

The "Green Fairy" has once again captured the attention of mixologists and sippers around the world. No other spirit in the western hemisphere has stimulated the imagination, engendered fear in the hearts of government officials, or fulfilled the promise of providing the consumer with a unique experience as absinthe. Gwydion Stone takes us on a journey through absinthe's two-century-old history to determine what this potion can offer cocktail lovers today.

*Looming like a succubus in shadowed, febrile dreams,
absinthe awaits you patiently; she knows you will come
to her. As all who explore the world of spirits—eventually,
inexorably—you will be drawn to the Emerald Muse...*

NO DRINK throughout history has inspired more allure, fear and awe than absinthe. That's no small accomplishment considering that its prime years spanned only several decades and its life, from birth to ban, spanned little more than a century, but what a century it was! The end of the eighteenth century in France, the cultural center of Europe at the time, saw the emergence of a vibrant philosophical spirit in salons, cafés and clubs—a spirit which in turn inspired and empowered the French people to rise up and overthrow a cruel and oppressive regime. The nineteenth century, although politically turbulent, culminated in a grand celebration of creative expression and joie de vivre that would span two decades: La Belle Époque—the Beautiful Times.

The mythopoetic power of absinthe cannot be denied. To the uninitiated, absinthe is often imagined to be some kind of deeply exotic, alchemical serum with potent hallucinogenic and aphrodisiac properties. Frequently mentioned alongside of opium, LSD and more recently ecstasy, absinthe is sometimes wrongly named "the acid of the Belle Époque," but seldom by anyone who has ever had it. Not surprisingly, the truth lies far from the myth, and the truth is that Absinthe is little more than a refreshing and exhilarating herbal liquor that can be compared to ouzo, raki, and Chartreuse.

Absinthe Known, Absinthe Inferred, Absinthe-Wished-For

When examining such a legendary and sensational topic, a historian will remain aware that there are three essential identities involved: the subject as known, the subject as inferred by historical remains, and the subject as-wished-for; i.e., as it has entered and been interpreted by the imagination and popular culture of the present time.

Fortunately for those who care to look for it, there exists an abundance of historical and modern evidence of the true nature of this drink. In fact, from time to time bottles of vintage, pre-ban absinthe will surface, still sealed, sometimes in near-mint condition. These have been subjected to modern scientific analysis—not to mention the scrutiny of educated palates—and are again being manufactured by commercial and non-commercial distillers alike. There also exists many contemporary accounts by those who not only imbibed absinthe, but some by those who manufactured it. We know precisely how pre-ban absinthe was made and, in some cases, by what recipes. It should also be noted that in secluded valleys of rural Switzerland, clandestine bootleggers have been making absinthe continuously since the ban.

All this notwithstanding, absinthe has maintained a mythical status in the popular mind, attended by some of the most outrageous, inaccurate and sometimes perplexing notions.

Absinthe Known

What is absinthe?

Although wormwood-infused drinks have been used in medicine for thousands of years, when we speak of "absinthe" nowadays, we are evoking a very specific spirituous liquor that rose to popularity in France and Switzerland beginning in the late eighteenth century.

To put it concisely: Absinthe is an anise-flavored aperitif distilled from anise, fennel and wormwood. Authentic absinthe is usually either green or clear, that is verte or blanche. When colored green, other herbs are used after distillation—as much for their flavoring and aromatic properties as for color. It is their chlorophyll that gives the peridot green hue for which absinthe is famous and which earned it the sobriquet, *La Fée Verte*—The Green Fairy. There is one known instance that has very recently come to light of a pre-ban rouge, or red absinthe. Little more is known of it so far than the simple fact that it existed, as shown by an advertising poster from the era.

Although absinthe is often referred to as a liqueur, this is not wholly accurate, as liqueurs are pre-sweetened and often somewhat syrupy. Absinthe is not pre-sweetened and is somewhat astringent and mildly bitter, but nowhere near as bitter as popular imagination would have it; not even so much as unsweetened tea.

Absinthe takes its name from its principle ingredient, grand wormwood, whose botanical name is *Artemisia absinthium*. Absinthe is the French word for the wormwood plant; the full proper name of the liquor, *Extrait d'Absinthe*, simply translates as "Wormwood Extract". Other traditional ingredients include petite wormwood (*Artemisia pontica*), melissa (*Melissa officinalis*) and hyssop (*Hyssopus officinalis*).

Absinthe is made by macerating the herbs for a brief time in 85 percent spirit; this mixture is then distilled, carrying the fragrant, volatile herbal oils into the liquor, leaving the vegetal matter and undesirable bitter compounds behind in the still. Absinthe is generally found in the proof range of 55 to 74 percent alcohol and is expressed in degrees of proof equivalent to alcohol percentage, i.e. 55 degrees equals 55 percent alcohol by volume.

In spite of internet and popular culture claims to the contrary, absinthe cannot be made at home from a kit by soaking herbs in spirits. This can be compared to soaking barley in spirits to make whiskey or adding grape Kool-Aid™ to diluted neutral spirits to make wine.

Absinthe Preparation

Absinthe is drunk as a simple cocktail. Proper preparation consists of very slowly diluting it with dripping iced water—whether dripping from a specially made absinthe fountain, or by hand from a carafe—to a ratio of approximately three to five parts water to one part absinthe, and sweetened to taste.

The tools and procedure for classic absinthe preparation. (From the collection of Gwydion Stone.)

A measure of absinthe, around 1 to 1.5 ounces, is poured into a glass. Absinthe glasses were, and are, often made to indicate the level of a proper "dose." Lacking an absinthe glass, a properly sized wine or water glass will do. Then a flat, perforated trowel-like absinthe spoon is placed on top of the glass and a sugar cube placed on top of the spoon. The perforations allow the water and melting sugar to pass into the glass of absinthe below.

The slow addition of water causes the herbal oils to gradually come out of suspension and the drink takes on a turbulent, cloudy, and opalescent louche. A good louche—not too thin, not too opaque—is a point upon which absinthes are judged.

Although some purists frown upon it, ice may be added. This should be taken into account while determining the dilution ratio and when pouring.

Origins

Legend has it that absinthe, as we know it, first saw light in Switzerland, dripping from the small still of an exiled French doctor by the name of Pierre Ordinaire, in 1792. This was just three years after the storming of the Bastille and the beginning of the French Revolution.

Although there is scant evidence of his actual existence, Dr. Ordinaire is an indispensable fixture in the legend of absinthe. Pernod Fils reports in their catalog from 1896:

> We cannot resist the urge to reproduce the portrait drawn of him by a Swiss writer. He was, apparently, an eccentric, of great height, riding through the Val de Travers on a small Corsican horse known in region as the Rocket. His unusual appearance did not fail to surprise the village populations; it gave rise to many jokes and persistent astonishment among the children. Ordinaire did not appear to be concerned with this; the gravity of his character was not affected. He was a doctor not without talents for his time, and he did a good job of bringing the medical art to the Val de Travers. He joined the practice of medicine to that of pharmacology; the majority of doctors of the countryside did no differently. Mr. Ordinaire did not scorn the panaceas; he employed one

in particular, the elixir of wormwood, composed of aromatic plants of which only he knew the secret. Many people, having made use of it, declared themselves radically cured and the doctor could not pretend to be other than pleased and to prescribe its use. Dr. Ordinaire would have been well astonished if anyone had predicted the high destinies to which his elixir would be called. At his death the mysterious recipe passed into the hands of the young Henriod ladies of Couvet. Cultivating the necessary herbs themselves in their garden, they distilled them in the family home. The production of the elixir at the time amounted only to a few pots, which were sold with some difficulty by hawking. Little by little, however, thanks to its fragrance and pleasant taste, the elixir came to the attention of not only the sick, but to that of more and more fans, so that the recipe had already acquired monetary value when Mr. Henri Louis Pernod acquired it to exploit it commercially.

According to one Swiss version of this legend, it was the Henriod sisters who were the original inventors and Ordinaire was a scoundrel who stole the formula, selling it to a Major Dubied, whose son-in-law was Henri Pernod.

There exists a Latin alchemical treatise on wormwood dating from 1667 that appears to give details on the distillation of a spirituous liquor containing the very ingredients we know as the herb bill of a traditional absinthe. It is still being translated at this writing, but it appears to be the earliest known record of distilled absinthe.

Although we will likely never know the exact origins of the very first absinthe ever distilled or the name of its inventor, the beginnings of commercial absinthe are pretty well documented.

It began with Abram-Louis Perrenoud, a distiller by trade, living in Couvet in the Val de Travers region of Switzerland. Somewhere around the year 1794, Abram-Louis scribbled this recipe in his diary:

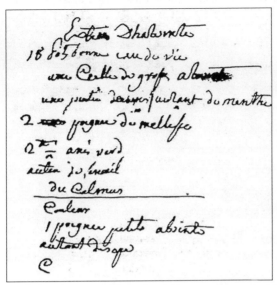

The original absinthe recipe Abram-Louis Perrenoud wrote in his diary.
(From the collection of Gwydion Stone.)

It reads:

Extract of Absinthe

For 18 pots of eau-de vie, (approximately 34 litres)
a large bucket of grand wormwood,
some mint,
2 handfuls of lemon balm
2 of green anise
same amount of fennel
some calamus.

Colour:
1 handful of petite wormwood
same amount of hyssop.

The formulation gained regional popularity not merely as a tonic, ostensibly its intended purpose, but as a beverage in its own right.

Major Daniel-Henri Dubied, a lace merchant with no distilling experience, recognized the commercial potential of the formula and purchased the recipe from Perrenoud, employing Abram-Louis's son Henri-Louis, who had learned the distilling trade from his father. In 1798, along with Dubied's sons, they began producing absinthe under the name of Dubied Père et Fils. In 1805, permutations of partnership, Henri-Louis changed his surname from Perrenoud to Pernod and he established a distillery of his own in Pontarlier, France: Pernod Fils.

Over the next 110 years many brands, some extraordinary and many substandard, came and went. Pernod Fils remained the standard to which all aspired—or chose to imitate.

ABSINTHE INFERRED

Absinthe Feared

So how did absinthe gain its notoriety? What led to this drink being banned almost globally? Politics, of course.

At first absinthe was a fairly expensive commodity, indulged in primarily by the upper middle class, but by the latter part of the 1800s several factors collided to bring absinthe into strong competition with wine as the national beverage—in a country famous for its wine.

At the time, wine was known to be natural and healthy and hence, spirits produced from wine—eau de vie, marc, brandy—were thought to be healthier and superior to less expensive spirits produced from beet sugar or grains. For this reason, absinthe producers preferred grape spirits to other alcohol. Whether grape spirits produce a better absinthe remains a topic for debate among absintheurs today.

When a phyloxera (tiny, aphid-like root lice) epidemic decimated the grape crops of France toward the end of the nineteenth century, wine prices—and hence, grape spirits prices—soared. Most manufacturers of absinthe switched to the cheaper alcohols out of economic necessity while others—most notably Pernod Fils—used the fact that they continued to use grape spirits to assert that their product was healthier as well as superior to that of their competitors. This also justified continuing to charge premium prices for premium absinthe. The effect of all this was that suddenly many absinthes were cheaper than wine, and at a much higher proof.

No longer exclusively the drink of the upper classes, absinthe was more accessible to the working man and in particular, as we well know, the "bohemians." The bohemians were self-impoverished artists, writers, musicians, free-thinkers and counter-culture types—essentially the beatniks, hippies, or punks of the era. These are the "famous absinthe drinkers" we hear so much about: Rimbaud, Verlaine, Toulouse-Lautrec, Satie, Debussy, Van Gogh, Gauguin, etc.

Bohemianism was actually something of a movement, peopled with "cultural gypsies" who had seceded from the conventional lifestyle in pursuit of "Truth, Beauty, Freedom and Love" as it was so aptly put in Baz Luhrmann's 2001 film, *Moulin Rouge*. The term "bohemian" was used because at the time it was erroneously believed that gypsies had originally come from Bohemia.

Although it no doubt approached the status of a sacrament to many of these figures, absinthe has become particularly associated with them more than others simply because it was they who chronicled its role in their lives and work; lives and work which were extraordinary enough to merit a place in history.

With the ubiquity of inexpensive absinthe, the bohemians, and nearly everyone else, indulged themselves enthusiastically, so enthusiastically in fact that alcoholism began to be a serious problem in France.

At the same time, less scrupulous manufacturers were cutting corners even further by adding poisonous adulterants such as copper sulfate for coloring and antimony chloride to enhance the louche. These no doubt contributed in part to the reported harmful effects of absinthe and it is perhaps because of this that the gathering enemies of absinthe coined a whole new social disease: absinthism.

The Myth of Absinthism

Charles Dudley Warner wrote in 1870: "Politics makes strange bedfellows." He was writing of his alliance with Harriet Beecher Stowe in support of the abolition of slavery, but he might as well have been referring to the parallel visions of two normally opposing factions: the powerful lobbyists of the now-recovering wine industry and the growing temperance and prohibitionist movements. Absinthe, their common adversary, was doomed.

With both sides arguing that absinthe brought its own unique health hazards, a myth was born.

The myth was largely the work of Dr. Valentin Magnan. His flawed studies on the effects of absinthe would be considered bad science by today's standards and they also received criticism from his peers at the time. The fact remains however that these were the formative work behind the assumptions and superstitions that many—including the FDA—cling to even today.

Absinthism, he claimed, was marked by hyperexcitability, epileptiform convulsions, hallucinations and addiction:

In absinthism, the hallucinating delirium is most active, most terrifying, sometimes provoking reactions of an extremely violent and dangerous nature. Another more grave syndrome accompanies this: all of a sudden the absinthist cries out, pales, loses consciousness and falls; the features contract, the jaws clench, the pupils dilate, the eyes roll up, the limbs stiffen, a jet of urine escapes, gas and waste material are brusquely expulsed. In just a few seconds the face becomes contorted, the limbs twitch, the eyes are strongly convulsed, the jaws gnash and the tongue projected between the teeth is badly gnawed; a bloody saliva covers the lip, the face grows red, becomes purplish, swollen; the eyes are bulging, tearful, the respiration is loud, then the movements cease, the whole body relaxes, the sphincter releases, the evacuations soil the sick man. Suddenly he lifts his head and casts his eyes around him with a look of bewilderment. Coming to himself after awhile, he doesn't remember one thing that has happened.

That will get your attention.

In order to reproduce the symptoms observed in "absinthists" in laboratory animals, Dr. Magnan used pure wormwood oil extract in his experiments, not commercially made, finished absinthe, which contains only a small amount of the herbal oils. This can be compared to doing a study on the effects of daily coffee drinking by feeding animals gargantuan doses of pure caffeine, the equivalent of 200 cups daily.

The British medical journal, *The Lancet*, published a number of articles about absinthe throughout the Belle Époque. In 1868:

> WE think it time that an authoritative and exhaustive inquiry should be made as to the effects of excessive absinthe drinking, about which a great deal is being said just now, not merely by medical men, but by the public. It is quite clear that a great deal of what has been said is mere nonsense, and will not bear a moment's investigation. And when one reads carefully even the seemingly authoritative description of the symptoms given by M. Legrand…it is impossible to fix on any definite peculiarities which clearly distinguish poisoning with absinthe from poisoning with any other

concentrated alcohol, taken in small doses repeated with extreme frequency…

For our own part, we have never been convinced that there is anything in the symptoms of acute or chronic absinthism as they are described, essentially different from those of acute or chronic alcoholism which has been produced by the imbibition of innumerable drams of any spirit.

We have repeatedly seen the whole train of symptoms, which are now so much talked of, produced by the constant drinking of brandy or rum. As for hallucinations, there is nothing more common. At any rate, it will take a good deal of very solid and precise evidence to convince us that the trifling amount of essence of wormwood contained in the liquor called absinthe, adds any considerable poisonous power to the natural influence of some 20 or 30 ounces per diem of a highly concentrated alcohol,

And again in 1869:

The question whether absinthe exerts any special action other than that of alcohol in general, has been revived by some experiments by MM. Magnan and Bouchereau in France. These gentlemen placed a guinea-pig under a glass case with a saucer full of essence of wormwood (which is one of the flavoring matters of absinthe) by his side. Another guinea-pig was similarly shut up with a saucer full of pure alcohol. A cat and a rabbit were respectively enclosed along with a saucer each full of wormwood. The three animals which inhaled the vapours of wormwood experienced, first, excitement, and then epileptiform convulsions. The guinea-pig which merely breathed the fumes of alcohol, first became lively, then simply drunk. Upon these facts it is sought to establish the conclusion that the effects of excessive absinthe drinking are seriously different from those of ordinary alcoholic intemperance.

The particular compound which excited the attention of scientists and critics was thujone, a terpene found in the volatile oil of wormwood—as well as in sage, rosemary, thyme, tansy, white cedar, tarragon, lavender, and a number of other herbs and botanicals commonly used in kitchens around the world.

In high enough doses, thujone is a potent neuro-toxin shown to produce hallucinations, epileptiform convulsions, brain damage, and renal failure. Fortunately, the trace amounts found in authentic absinthe and other foods are far below what would be considered hazardous. Since virtually any substance is subject to abuse, and any chemical compound consumed in excess will be found to be toxic or damaging, it is likely that thujone was nothing more than the scapegoat sought, found, and exploited.

It is also important to remember that, in French, the word "absinthe" may be used for the plant and the essential extracts as well as the drink. This permitted no small amount of abuse by anti-absinthe lobbyists when quoting Magnan's and other scientists' findings.

In the end we find that the entire basis for the current dark reputation of absinthe was formed by political manipulation, moralistic propaganda, and the bad science used to serve them. We have seen more recent examples of this phenomenon in the treatment of other recreational substances subject to abuse.

Absinthe Banned

The work of the temperance leagues and incompetent or dishonest scientists was not without effect. As the problem of alcoholism grew, so did the accompanying crime and other social issues associated with it. Whenever a violent crime was committed, if any connection to absinthe could be made, it was seized upon as proof of the demonic influence of the Green Devil.

This all came to a head in Switzerland in 1905 when a man named Jean Lanfray, in a drunken rage, murdered his pregnant wife and two daughters and then attempted to kill himself. Of course, Lanfray was an absinthiste—an absinthe addict. It was pointed out that he had had two glasses of absinthe prior to the murders. What was not pointed out was that he was an habitual drunkard who drank any kind of alcohol that he could get his hands on, and that he would consume as much as five liters of wine a day. He had drunk the two absinthes that morning before going to work. He had also drunk a crème de menthe, a cognac, six glasses of wine at lunch, another glass of wine before leaving work; at home, a cup of coffee with brandy, a liter of wine and then another coffee with marc in it. Undoubtedly it was the absinthe, taken hours earlier, which pushed him over the edge.

Shortly after the Lanfray incident petitions were circulated and the public began increasingly to adopt the position that absinthe was a menace; a position based on media manipulation and misinformation, and which also fattened the larders of the wine industry.

Absinthe was banned in Switzerland in 1910, in the USA in 1912, and finally in France in 1915. With the Green Fairy in exile and WWI escalating, the spell was broken and the Belle Époque had come to an end.

Absinthe As Wished For

Thujone gets a lot of sensational press on the fringes of the absinthe world. Given the events of the cusp of the 1960s and 1970s, warnings about hallucinations strike a familiar note to the hopeful "inner-space" explorer—in fact that seems to be the one bit of information upon which many focus, blithely ignoring the foaming at the mouth, explosive incontinence and the seizures.

So begins the invention of the idea of absinthe as a psychedelic recreational drug and talk of absinthe's "secondary effects."

However exaggerated and spurious they may have been, it seems that the early health warnings were taken as a sort of code: "We only forbid this substance because it will get you high and free your mind." Perhaps this is partly because warnings of this type have been issued over virtually every substance that has been deemed suitable for recreational use and/or consciousness alteration. In the popular and uninformed imagination, absinthe is a dark and forbidden addictive drug, like opium, perhaps consumed in "absinthe dens."

This confusion was not helped when, in 1975, scientists J. del Castillo, M. Anderson, and G.M. Rubottom suggested that the geometric similarity between the thujone molecule and that of tetrahydrocannabinol (THC), the active component in marijuana, might indicate similar effects by activating the same receptors in the brain. Even though this was demonstrated not to be the case as early as 1978 and again in 1998, you will still find this misinformation repeated as fact in magazine and newspaper articles, on internet forums and web sites and private discussion. Thujone is fetishized by those seeking a new exotic high. It's more fun than the truth, which is that absinthe is just booze, doesn't actually contain much thujone, and it never did.

Unless one makes a study of it, one is unlikely to know just how omni-present absinthe was at its height of popularity. Let's imagine for a moment the scene in France at the turn of the century. There were over 30,000 cafés in Paris alone. The drink of favor was absinthe, which throngs of people congregated to imbibe every day at 5:00 P.M., giving this "happy hour" period the nickname *l'heure verte*, the

181

"green hour". Are we really expected to believe that the majority of the drinking population of France was sitting around in cafés every day, hallucinating on absinthe?

THE "SECONDARY" EFFECT

So what is the secondary absinthe effect that one hears so much about?

Some people—but not all—have observed a very subtle and short-lived "buzz" when drinking authentic absinthe. It is usually described as a sort of mental clarity or a "clear-headed" drunk: whereas most liquor produces a slower, thicker mental state, absinthe seems to contain a balanced stimulant effect. When one would normally be slurring and weaving and nodding off after too much bourbon, one is likely to be still quite convivial, bright and alert after a few absinthes. This is not to say one doesn't get every bit as intoxicated from absinthe. Over-indulgence quickly replaces this clarity with the more familiar deleterious effects of any alcohol.

It appears that the relaxing and disinhibiting effects of alcohol are complimented by the stimulation and lightness thought to result from the particular combination of herbs. Modern research suggests that it is the combination of herbal ingredients, more particularly the fenchone from the fennel and the anethol from the anise, which works in synergy with the other ingredients to produce this effect. The author has experienced a "secondary effect" identical to that of absinthe, from drinking a liquor made from fennel alone. It should be repeated that not everyone experiences "secondaries" and that some believe them to be nothing more than the placebo effect.

Absinthe wasn't banned everywhere. It remained legal in the UK, Spain, and Eastern Europe. Of course that's probably because it was never very popular there and was never perceived as being a problem. Still, absinthe production dwindled and by the mid 1900s had all but disappeared.

After a period of forty years of relative obscurity, during which the reputation of absinthe took on a shape more appropriate to an urban legend, the Green Fairy was ready to re-emerge from her cocoon, twisted into a most unlikely and—to anyone who knew her—unrecognizable form. In the Czech Republic in 1990, just after the Velvet Revolution and the return of privately owned enterprise, a small distillery began producing what it called "absinth."

According to its official history, Hill's Liguere was established in 1920 by Albin Hill. He starting out as a wine wholesaler and soon after began producing his own liquor and liqueurs. In 1947, his son Radomil opened his own branch of the business and it was then that they began producing "absinth," 160 proof Alpsky Rum and *ubrówka* (bison grass vodka, "good for the sex drive!"). The next year the communist regime took over and seized the distillery, putting the Hills out of work. After the revolution in 1990, Radomil, having successfully negotiated for the return of his property, began producing Hill's Absinth.

It should be noted that although there exists much absinthe related art and antiques from all over France and Switzerland from before the bans a hundred years ago—glasses, spoons, advertising posters, menus, distillers' catalogs and invoices, books and distillation manuals, antique absinthe bottles of many brands, paintings depicting absinthe and absinthe drinkers—there is so far nothing which suggests that Hill's absinth existed prior to 1990.

The liquor is a very pale turquoise blue and bears no resemblance to absinthe. It contains little or no anise and does not louche when water is added. Tests have suggested that it possibly contains no wormwood and its peculiar minty flavor has been compared to mouthwash. It is almost certainly an "oil mix," meaning that essential oils are simply mixed with a neutral alcohol base, artificially colored and then bottled rather being distilled from natural herbs, as an authentic absinthe would be. By all appearances Hill, knowing that precious few people in his market knew anything about what absinthe should be like, and very likely not knowing himself, simply concocted an odd-tasting liquor and dubbed it "absinth." Subsequent Czech imitators came up with similar inventions and worse: noting that bitterness was among the words used to describe pre-ban absinth, they conjectured that it should be terribly, terribly bitter. Consequently, many Czech absinths are.

Nonetheless, Hill's absinth made its way into the bars and rock clubs of the Czech Republic, especially Prague, where it was discovered by the metal, darkwave and punk set—the bohemians of our time; and where better than Bohemia itself? In some cases, confusion of the essentially unrelated nineteenth century French use of the term "bohemian" has been opportunistically used to validate the lineage of Czech absinth.

Part of the romance and interest of authentic absinthe lay in its ritualistic preparation—the sugar cube and the special spoon; the dripping water; watching the louche develop and smelling the herbal fragrances bloom. Unfortunately, Czech absinth doesn't louche. A new element was necessary to make the paraphernalia relevant.

No doubt borrowing the preparation of the Café Brûlot, a traditional coffee drink where a brandy or cognac-soaked sugar lump is ignited in a spoon before adding it to the coffee, people began lighting absinth-soaked sugar on fire

before dumping it in their drink along with the water. This
makes for an initially interesting and dramatic display, as
any flambé will, but the burnt sugar adhering to the spoon,
the indissoluble globs at the bottom of the glass, and the
introduced charred taste of carbonized sugar will leave a
true absintheur cold. Of course this ritual also calls to mind
the preparation of heroin by cooking it in a spoon; another
unfortunate connection with illicit and dangerous drugs.

With very few exceptions, Czech absinths are considered to be inferior, and in most cases outright fraudulent
imitations of authentic absinthe.

ABSINTHE TODAY

As unfortunate as the events which led to the re-
emergence of absinthe may be, it is fortunate that they
occurred, because they created the market and the interest
which inspired French and Swiss distillers, both legal and
clandestine, to pressure their governments and the new
European Union to re-examine the case against absinthe.
As a result, many countries, especially France and Switzerland have reformed their absinthe laws and absinthe is
again being legally produced there.

Several old absinthe distilleries, those of Pierre Guy,
Paul Devoilles and Emile Pernot, are again producing
quality, old-style absinthe by the same methods, recipes
and ingredients as they formerly had done. Also, new
distillers are joining the trade. Most notable among these
is Jade Liqueurs.

WHAT TO LOOK FOR IN A GOOD ABSINTHE

Absinthe is judged by similar criteria as other spirits,
essentially: color, aroma, and taste. It should not be tasted

or drunk neat. Both the alcohol and the anise oils are too strong and will immediately disable your palate.

First, note the color, if any. Does it appear to be artificial, or is it most likely natural? Is it clear and bright, or hazy and throwing sediment?

Next, note the aroma before adding water. Does it merely smell strongly of alcohol, can you smell the herbs? Is it a rich, interesting, perfumed fragrance and do the herbs seem in balance; or does one overwhelm the others? Is it one-dimensional and unremarkable? When adding water the volatile oils come out of suspension and more of their fragrant properties are released. The aroma should "bloom" with more complexity.

Also as water is added, watch the absinthe louche. Does it develop gradually and gracefully or does it begin to louche almost instantly? Is it thin and watery or thick and milky? A good louche should come on slowly and develop a rich and creamy look, but still have a slight translucent, opalescent appearance when viewed in good light. Full sun is the best place to observe the louche. The color should be interesting and jewel-like, not flat and dull.

How does it feel in your mouth? Mouth-feel is a good indicator of quality ingredients and good production technique. It should feel rich, creamy, and smooth, not excessively astringent and dry.

How does it taste? Drinking absinthe should remind you of walking through an alpine meadow on a late spring day. It should be cool, crisp, clean, and refreshing; not heavy, oily or overly bitter. It should taste neither medicinal nor mouthwash-like. It should taste well balanced and interesting, not one-dimensional. While absinthe is an anise drink, it should not taste like black licorice candy, but have more of the other herbs showing up as well.

Common flaws are:

Too bitter. This often arises from the mistake of using the wrong type of wormwood in the post-distillation coloration. Too much star anise also gives an unusual, dry bitterness. Absinthe should be no more bitter than tea.

Too minty. This is a big problem with Czech and Eastern European products. While mint can be used to advantage, if you can easily detect the characteristic cool, mint taste, it's probably too much.

Camphorous. This is the result of using of the wrong type of fennel. Only Florence fennel should be used. Common fennel is not the same species.

Too much anise. Some of the lower quality French absinthes rely on too much star anise to get a good louche, at the expense of producing an almost chemical candy-like character.

Too little anise. This is mostly a problem with the Czech products, but also some of the French ones. Czechs prefer to avoid anise altogether, thus bypassing the classic flavor profile of proper absinthe. Some French brands simply use too little to get a good louche and full flavor.

ABSINTHE ACQUIRED

While the sale and importation of absinthe into the US is still prohibited by the FDA, it is successfully ordered online by many absintheurs from several reputable and reliable distributors. Of course there is always a risk of seizure by customs, but this is fairly uncommon. Absinthe is not scheduled by the DEA as a controlled substance, but is merely "prohibited merchandise," similar to a turtle shell brought back from the Virgin Islands. State laws vary about possession of spirits upon which taxes or duty have not been paid and the shipping of spirits in general. Seizure from luggage at airports is more common, but appears to be subject to the caprice and knowledge of the individual agent.

Four distributors stand well out from the rest as carrying a superior line of products as well as guaranteeing delivery:

Liqueurs de France
www.absintheonline.com
Absinthe Distribution
www.absinthe-distribution.com
Fine Spirits Corner
www.spiritscorner.com
The Frenchman
www.absinthefrenchmanspoon.com

BIBLIOGRAPHY

Code of Federal Regulations. Title 21, Volume 3. CITE: 21CFR172.510 (Revised as of April 1, 2004).

Baker, Phil. 2001. *The Book of Absinthe: A Cultural History*. New York: Grove Press.

Delahaye, Marie-Claude. 2005. *PERNOD: 200 ans d'entreprise: l'Absinthe dictionnaire des marques*. Auvers-sur-Oise: Musée de l'Absinthe.

Lachenmeier, Dirk W., J. Emmert, T. Kuballa, and G. Sartor. 2006. "Thujone—Cause of absinthism?" *Forensic Science International* 158 (1): 1-8. [E-pub ahead of print (May 17, 2005), http://ist-socrates.berkeley.edu/~mcb165/lachenmeier_2005_thujone.pdf.]

Lancet, The. 1868. "Absinthe." 91 (2332): 600-601.

Lancet, The. 1869. "Absinthe and Alcohol." 93 (2375): 317-354.

Magnan, Valantin. 1874. "On the Comparative Action of Alcohol and Absinthe." *The Lancet* 104 (2664): 410-412.

Meschler, Justin P. and Allyn C. Howlett. 1999. "Thujone Exhibits Low Affinity for Cannabinoid Receptors But Fails to Evoke Cannabimimetic Responses." *Pharmacology Biochemistry and Behavior* 62 (3): 473-480.

Nathan-Maister, David. 2005. *Oxygenée's Virtual Absinthe Museum,*
www.oxygenee.com

Noël, Benoit, Peter Verte, and Artemis. 2003. *Absinthe: A Myth Always Green.* Paris: l'Esprit frappeur.

United States Code, TITLE 19 - CHAPTER 4 - SUBTITLE III - Part V - Sec. 1595. - Searches and seizures

The Spirit
of the Bat

A BRIEF HISTORY OF BACARDI RUMS

BY ROBERT HESS

Few spirits can weave a tale of that crossed oceans, influenced world economy, and triggered a revolution quite like rum. The world's most popular rum, Bacardi, also has a story to tell of invention, family pride, revolution, and a landmark court case the Robert Hess presents for your consideration.

CHRISTOPHER COLUMBUS may be credited with discovering the Americas, but few realize that he was also the father of rum, even though he never really knew it himself.

Spirits are made by taking fermented product (fruits or grains, with a maximum alcohol potential of around 17 percent) and applying science to increase the alcohol to a desired level. Fermentation occurs when yeasts eat the sugars contained in the base product, producing alcohol and carbon dioxide as by-products. Fruits have relatively easy-to-access sugars. When fermented and distilled, they produce brandy. The internal sugars in grains are a little trickier to expose, and thus need to be germinated and malted. But if the core of this process revolves around giving those hungry little yeasts a sugar feast, then why don't the distillers just feed them sugar directly? You can, they do, and they make rum.

Rum has a long and mostly turbulent history amongst the islands scattered throughout the Caribbean Sea, dating back to Columbus's second voyage in 1493.

A native to New Guinea, sugarcane grew well in various parts of the Old World—China, India, Arabia, Africa, Spain, the Canary Islands—and provided a good source of sugar used for various culinary and confectionary purposes. When Columbus landed on Haiti in search of gold, he had also brought with him sugarcane from the Canary Islands. The natives were forced to cultivate and harvest this newly introduced crop and eventually to process it into sugar.

In 1506, the first molasses was extracted on the island of Puerto Rico, using an Indian *cunyaya* to wring out the cane juice. Ten years later, the first New World sugarcane mill was established in the Dominican Republic. By the late 1500s, sugarcane production spread through the rest of the Caribbean. Some people say that capitalism was born in the 1600s from the export of sugar from the New World: the Infernal Triangle.

Sugar made the New World prosper. But molasses was in much lower demand than sugar. Frankly, it wasn't worth the cost to ship it back to the Old World, and so it was simply discarded or used as fertilizer or cattle feed.

Call it inspiration or luck, but sometime during the early 1600s, African slaves—imported to work in the cane fields—discovered that molasses fermented into a crude beer. Then at some point a colonist with a still, a common enough piece of equipment, took the brew and distilled it into alcohol: rum was invented. By 1627, the British colonists were producing rum in Barbados. After all, one acre of sugarcane produced enough molasses to make 200 gallons of rum. The plantation owners continued to profit from sugar, while rum producers found "white gold" in the sticky, black by-product that no one wanted.

At the time, however, this new income source wasn't called rum. Instead it went by a few different names, like "Kill Devil," a reference to rum's supposed medicinal properties. The local natives believed rum had the ability to drive out evil spirits.

An anonymous manuscript from around 1650, entitled "Description of Barbados," provided the following: "The chief fuddling they make in the island is Rumbullion, alias Kill-Divil [sic], and this is made of sugar canes distilled, a hot, hellish, and terrible liquor." Few would describe this as a positive accounting of the islands, or of what would eventually become one of their most famous exports.

The British sailors discovered rum for themselves when the Royal Navy captured Jamaica in 1655. Ships were given rum at a deep discount because the navy's presence discouraged pirates from invading the islands. It soon became a routine practice on board ship to dole out 2.5 pints of rum to each sailor, each day. Even though it might not be of superb quality, it was strong, it was cheaper and better than beer, and it didn't spoil on long voyages.

On August 21, 1740, Vice Admiral Edward Vernon modified this ration by adding a quart of water and lime juice. His nickname was "Old Grogram," owing to the grogram coat he always wore on ship, and the resulting ration became commonly known as "Grog."[106] This would remain a standard component of the Royal Navy until July 31, 1970.

The British Navy, which pretty much ruled the seas in those days, added rum to its stockpile of products, which traveled to the Old and New Worlds alike. However, rum didn't quite catch on with the tipplers in Europe. This product of the sugar cane was far harsher than the brandies, wines, and beers that they were more comfortable with. The New World, on the other hand, was a different story.

Rum, despite its harsh nature, became quite popular amongst the colonists, probably owing at least partly to the fact that it was cheaper and easier to obtain than spirits, which needed to be imported from Europe. Over time, the rum distillers learned the craft of barrel aging; originating perhaps from the need to store product that awaited shipment. Aging in barrel produced a side effect: the rum took on color from the wood and some of its harsher qualities were filtered out.

---

106. UK Ministry of Defense, "On this day....21 August," Press Notice (online) http://www.mod.uk; no longer active. See also the FAQ section of the Royal Naval Museum website: http://www.royalnavalmuseum.org/visit_see_sailfaq.htm (accessed April 23, 2006).

But rum's popularity was not dependent on its taste or acceptability in the Old World. Rum spread northward to the American colonies and gained acceptance for another reason.

More profitable than the lumber and iron export trade, New England colonists began importing molasses and producing rum. The Dutch began producing rum on Staten Island in 1664. And three years later, Boston's first distillery was established.

During the 1700s, New England and Mid-Atlantic rum producers manufactured millions of gallons for traders who then exchanged the rum for slaves, who were then shipped off to the Caribbean sugarcane plantations. Costing 5 pence per gallon to produce, rum was easier and cheaper to trade for slaves than hard currency. An adult slave was purchased for 120 gallons of rum and sold in the Caribbean for £30-80.

With this boom in their economy, American colonists began purchasing even cheaper molasses from non-British colonies in the Spanish- and French-held Caribbean. Encouraged by growers in the British West Indies, the British Parliament passed the Molasses Act in 1733, imposing a sixpence tax per gallon on non-British sugar and molasses imported into the American colonies.

For a while, New England distillers skirted the tax by smuggling molasses and bribing officials. This didn't last long. In debt from the French and Indian War, Prime Minister George Grenville slashed the excise tax to 3 pence and added more goods to the importation duty list. American exports had to be bonded and the New England export trade in rum, lumber, and iron slacked, as did its importation of molasses, creating an economic depression.

The colonists took on an independent nature, and this Molasses Act was just the start in a long series of attempts by the British government to impose control over its far-off colony. Eventually, this led to the Revolutionary War, during which America broke free of Britain and formed an independent country and government.

A side effect of all of this activity was that the previously smoothly-run rum trade was severely disrupted. In true pioneer spirit, the colonists learned to fend for themselves. Since grain was a strong crop in the north, the Americans started making whiskey.

The Napoleonic Wars, which occurred in the early 1800s, likewise disrupted sugar trade between Europe and the Caribbean islands. This meant Europeans no longer had access to their much-loved product. Necessity brought about scientific research, resulting in a switch of sugar production in Europe from the sugar cane to the sugar beet, a product that was far easier and cheaper to grow. All of this held dire consequences for the once-great sugar plantations of the West Indies.

Caribbean rum, which had begun to show promise of improvement, suddenly fell upon cheaper and less-refined production methods to regain its market footing by providing a less expensive product. The result was that they became so vilified that what had once been named "Kill Devil" because of its ability to defy demons, now gained the nickname "Demon Rum," because of its status in society as an exceedingly inferior, as well as exceedingly cheap, source of inebriation. The Temperance Union and Prohibitionists used demon rum as a rallying point to combat drunken behavior in general, and drinking of any sort in particular.

It was at about this time that the most prominent name in rum was born. This name would play a major role in the revitalization of the Caribbean spirit.

Born in Sitges, Spain in 1814, Don Facundo Bacardi y Masso and his brothers immigrated to Cuba in 1829. There he learned the art of rum making at the John Nunes distillery in Santiago de Cuba. In 1862 Don Facundo purchased his former employer's facility and innocently established the Bacardi Distillery. It was not without purpose that Facundo and his brother José embarked upon this business venture. Fecundo felt he knew how to vastly improve the quality of the rums they produced. Armed with his new concept in rum production, he soon produced a product that could stand toe-to-toe with the best spirits of the world. In addition to using the already established process of aging rum in barrels, he added the step of charcoal filtering to remove further impurities and create far smoother rum then had otherwise been possible.

Legend has it that the distillery had a colony of fruit bats living in the rafters. A symbol of watchfulness and family harmony in Spanish culture, Don Facundo's wife, Doña Amalia Moreau, suggested that bottles of Bacardi rum should be labeled with an image of a bat. Since many of Bacardi's early customers were illiterate Cuban workers, the easily identifiable symbol of *el ron de murcielagos* ("the rum of the bats") readily took hold.

Almost immediately after the company was established, social and political problems escalated throughout Cuba. Such troubles were to play a major role in the future of this fledgling company. Cuba was a colony of Spain and, like America 100 years before, resentment grew amidst the Cuban population toward Spanish imperial rule. October 10, 1868, marked the beginning of the "Ten Year War," which pitted the Cuban resistance against the Spanish army. Unfortunately, things for the Cubans did not result in the freedom seen by their American neighbors. In 1878 the defeated Cuban rebels signed a treaty with Spain and their dream of freedom was gone.

The Bacardi family was caught in the middle of the politics of the war. Facundo Bacardi y Maso, a Spanish émigré, felt duty bound to his European homeland, but his Cuban-born children sided with the freedoms sought by the rebellion. The war further disrupted their lives, as the casualties of war included many of the sugar mills across the island. The Bacardi distillery's supply source was now thoroughly disrupted. Despite the war, Bacardi rum was represented, rather amazingly, at the 1876 Centennial Philadelphia Exposition, where it won a gold medal in its category, beating out all of the Jamaican rums (which until then were considered the best in the world). It was only a mere ten years later however, Facundo Bacardi y Maso died at the age of seventy-one.

THE TUMULTUOUS YEARS

The Bacardi Company, now under the joint ownership of Facundo's three sons, Emilio, Facundo, and José, continued to press forward with the attention to quality and expansion that their father had begun. In 1888, despite the strained politics between Cuba and Spain, Bacardi was appointed as purveyor to the Spanish royal household, and was given the right to bear the Spanish coat-of-arms on its products.

In 1892, after having won several gold medals for its rum, the Bacardi Company got further accolades to add to its list of achievements by way of Alfonso XIII, the king of Spain. Alfonso was born in 1886 and was a sickly child. It was during one of his infirmities that he fell ill with the grippe, and, for whatever reason, the Royal physicians chose to administer Bacardi rum as a curative. That evening the young prince had his first restful sleep in days, and his fever soon broke. News of Bacardi spread.

Then in February 1895 the Cuban War of Independence began another ten-year period that introduced constant, disruptive changes in the face of the Cuban government. America got involved in the war on the Cuban side due, in part, to the bombing of the US battleship Maine in Havana harbor. This resulted in the temporary occupation of Cuba by the US, followed by a short-lived period of self-government; America was called in once more to take over in 1906 when opposition liberals sparked a serious revolt.

Emilio Bacardi, who had briefly served as Santiago's first popularly-elected mayor and then as a senator in Havana, returned home to Santiago to once more work with his brothers at the family company. After forty years of being in and around revolutionary politics, it was time for the Bacardi Company to cement its position as a premier provider of fine rums.

America's renewed awareness of and involvement with Cuba helped to further open markets for Bacardi's utilization and expansion. To help satisfy increased worldwide orders, in 1910 Bacardi opened up its first overseas factory in Barcelona, Spain. A year later, in 1911, the company finally upgraded its original alembic still, which had been producing rums for almost 73 years (the first 24 of which were for John Nunes). Through the increased capacity of its new still the company saw an explosion in demand for its rums. By 1916, Bacardi opened up a bottling plant in Manhattan to help fill the demands of a thirsty American audience.

Then Prohibition hit. While worldwide sales were not affected at all, the American market dried up. Despite this cut, there was an apparently unexplainable increase in orders coming from other parts of the world. On the books, Shanghai was the largest importer of Bacardi rums, although the orders most likely never actually made it to Shanghai. Even if the Bacardi Company had reason to suspect the shipping shenanigans that were going on, however, it wasn't its concern to make any fuss about them.

With the proximity of liquor-friendly Cuba to the now dry and liquor-unfriendly America, a large influx of American tourists began paying frequent visits. Havana became the unofficial saloon of America.

As Bacardi was the best selling spirit in Cuba, it quickly became the most popular spirit amongst the visiting Americans. Here they discovered such drinks as the Daiquiri, Mojito, Floridita, and the Bacardi Cocktail. While Bacardi rum was not well known in America prior to Prohibition, the returning tourists took home with them a memory and a taste for it, as well as for the drinks made with it.

Following Prohibition, Bacardi focused on officially renewing and growing its market in America. Prohibition had already seen an increase in the awareness and brand recognition of the product, but this also brought with it the bootleggers' use of questionable products that claimed to be Bacardi rum. So it was necessary for Bacardi to also re-assert its claim to the brand name and remind people what real Bacardi rum tasted like.

To better and more profitably provide rums to the US market, Bacardi opened up a facility in Puerto Rico in 1936. Rums produced in Puerto Rico, being a US territory, were not subject to import tariffs that were applied to rums imported from Cuba. This American expansion, when added to the company's new plants in Mexico and Barcelona, positioned Bacardi well to move its product throughout the world.

For 25 years, Bacardi continued to build up its company and establish its brand. Meanwhile, the politics of Cuba continued to evolve, and a government that at first appeared to be a welcome relief from Spanish rule and American occupation, eventually fell into disrepair through internal government corruption and power struggles. When, in 1958, a small rebel force began to form a resistance under the leadership of Fidel Castro, the Cuban population proved very welcoming. Over the next couple of years, the previous government fled and the Castro government took shape. A shape that very quickly turned from good, to bad, to worse.

Law 890

In October of 1960, Fidel Castro's new government passed Law 890, which instituted national control of over 400 different businesses across Cuba, including all of the Bacardi holdings. In one single moment, the Bacardi family lost over $76 million in property and assets that they had built up in their plants at Santiago and Havana. Over the course of the next couple of months, the Bacardi family, along with many of their workers, fled Cuba to focus their attentions on moving the seat of their manufacturing power to their other plants in Puerto Rico, New York, Mexico, and Nassau. It was almost a hundred years after Don Facundo Bacardi y Masso first established the Bacardi distillery in Cuba.

What had started as a modest little distillery in a tin-roofed shack had become an internationally known company, with interests and distilleries scattered across the world. It was to these foreign plants and holdings that the Bacardi family, and more importantly its trademark,

escaped. Through fortunate foresight, the Bacardi company charter gave it the necessary flexibility to move its
corporate offices quickly and easily off of Cuban soil. It was
thus that Bacardi headquarters took up official residence
in New York City.

Castro mistakenly thought he could take control of
Bacardi itself by seizing the physical manifestation of
Bacardi in Cuba. The spirit of Bacardi, however, existed
in its family, and the family wasn't willing to give up so
easily. They quickly set up the appropriate legal roadblocks
to prevent any rum produced in Cuba from being able to
use the Bacardi label.

This was a tough time for the family, but this adver-
sity made them stronger and more determined than ever
to survive as a company. They now had plants in Puerto
Rico, Mexico, and Brazil, with another plant already in the
planning stages for Nassau in the Bahamas. Mexico was
producing 1 million cases a year, Puerto Rico was producing almost that much, with 700,000 of those cases going
through the New York distribution office.

A New Life

It was during the 1960s that Bacardi took a radical
and innovative marketing step that spurred its growth and
worldwide recognition to the next level. The company
approached Coca-Cola and suggested a joint marketing
program in which Bacardi and Coke would promote the
Cuba Libre, but referring to it as "Bacardi and Coke." It
was through such successful marketing campaigns as this
that Bacardi bounced back from its Cuban exile and turned
what could have been a disaster for the company into yet
another chapter in its success.

By 1972, Bacardi had finished their new facility in Bermuda, and with it established the headquarters for Bacardi International. It is important to realize that the Bacardi company overall was not a single individual entity, but had in fact by this time been spread into five rather distinct corporate entities. In addition to "Bacardi International" in Bermuda, there was Bacardi Corporation, which was the main distillery in Puerto Rico; Bacardi Imports, which had originally been located in New York, and by this time had moved to Miami; Bacardi Mexico, which was the distillery in Mexico; and Bacardi & Company, which was located in Nassau and the legal holder of the trademark for the entire organization. These individual entities often played an important role in managing not only the various markets around the world, but also in providing beneficial tax breaks and incentives based on the nationalities that they were selling to. In America, the IRS was always paying special attention to the figures coming out of the Miami office and the Puerto Rico offices to make sure the government's appropriate due was being paid, especially since taxes taken from Puerto Rican businesses were diverted back to Puerto Rico, and not to the coffers of the 50 states.

As you can imagine, maintaining a complex worldwide organization is not an easy task, especially one that is also owned in its majority by a large and growing family. But success seemed to move the Bacardi family tree, and entering the 1980s, they saw spectacular growth. In each year of 1977, 1978, and 1979, Bacardi increased sales by 1 million cases. Prior to then, no other spirit brand had grown by 1 million cases a year, much less do it three years running. Bacardi now ranked seventh amongst America's largest importers and distributors; ahead of them were only Seagram, Heublein, National, Schenley, Hiram-Walker, and Brown-Forman. It is important to note that most of those

companies were focused on a broad portfolio of products,
while Bacardi was but a single brand.

The 1980s however proved to be a setback for not only Bacardi, but also the liquor industry in general. With both an increase in "health consciousness," as well as a renewed effort by various anti-alcohol organizations, public opinion began to sway against alcohol, which resulted in an industry wide slump. Sales of whiskey, and other brown spirits saw the decline sharpen, while the growth markets of the 1970s (rum and vodka) went flat. Concern amongst the Bacardi officers and family grew to focus on the fact that they were a one-product company, and therefore profitability could suffer if the general public moved away from that one product—rum.

In 1983, Bacardi took a gamble at diversification, and purchased Lloyd's Electronics: a gamble that failed, forcing Bacardi to sell that holding in 1985. Throughout the 1980s various movements towards diversification, both product-wise and organizational-wise, were discussed, attempted, or thwarted, with none of them bringing about the results that would prove profitable for the company.

Bacardi realized that is needed to streamline the structure and organization of the company to further its efforts toward advancing both its product and its name. In 1992, the five individual companies faced the realities of the global market strategy and established Bacardi Ltd in Hamilton, Bermuda, to be the central authority for the various Bacardi operations around the world. It was under this new organizational structure that Bacardi purchased Martini & Rossi in 1993, which began a successful phase of diversification into markets more closely aligned with what Bacardi was already familiar with—spirits. This diversification not only included many additional product brands, but in 1995 it also saw the introduction of Bacardi

Limon, the company's first flavored rum. This introduction was so successful, that over the years, several additional flavors were added to the growing lineup.

Today, Bacardi is the world's largest privately held spirits company, with its trademark line of rum selling more than 200 million bottles a year in nearly 200 countries. Its overall product portfolio has been increasing since that original purchase of Martini & Rossi to now include Bombay Sapphire, Dewar's Scotch, DiSaronno Amaretto, B&B, Grey Goose vodka, Cazadores tequila, and Noilly Pratt vermouth, just to name a few of the more then 250 labels within the Bacardi portfolio.

THE MIX

As a mixologist, it would be difficult for me to cover Bacardi, without also providing at least something in the way of a historical cocktail that involves their product. While drinks such as the Cuba Libre, Daiquiri, and Mojito might sound like obvious and well-known choices, I think I'd rather leave you with some details about the Bacardi Cocktail, a simple and refreshing drink that isn't really seen much these days.

During Prohibition, Bacardi became one of the brand-name distinctive products throughout the US, unfortunately many of the products being sold by that name were not in fact Bacardi rum, and in some cases not even rum at all. Following Prohibition, Bacardi was focused on not only leveraging the existing brand awareness that they had, but also preventing misuse of its name and brand.

One effort, which made it all the way to the New York Supreme Court, was the case of the Bacardi Cocktail. This drink was one of the most popular drinks during the '30s, you could sort of think of it as being the Cosmopolitan of the day. Unfortunately, it wasn't always a given that it would actually be made with Bacardi Rum. There was a hotel and restaurant chain that listed the Bacardi Cocktail on its menu, but in fact didn't use Bacardi rum in producing the drink. Following a long, and often entertaining, legal battle, Bacardi came out on top, with the clear ruling that only Bacardi rum could be used in making a Bacardi Cocktail. Here then is the recipe, as currently listed on the Bacardi website:

BACARDI COCKTAIL
1.5 ounce BACARDI Carta Blanca (Light-Dry) rum
1 ounce lime juice
0.5 teaspoon sugar
0.5 ounce grenadine
Mix in a shaker or blender with ice and strain into a chilled cocktail glass or serve on the rocks.

It is essentially a Daiquiri, but one that uses grenadine as part of its sweetening. While most grenadines today aren't much more then red-colored simple syrup, with a little bit of citric acid for tartness, real grenadine is made from pomegranates, and has a slightly more complex flavor from not only the pomegranate juice, but also from the seeds who provide just a hint of their flavor to the product as well.

If you'd like to make your own grenadine, try this recipe that I've slightly modified from one that I found on http://www.martiniplace.com:

HOME-MADE GRENADINE
2 cups sugar
2 cups water
2 pomegranates, seeded
2 ounces vodka
Simmer the sugar and water in a saucepan, stirring until the sugar is well dissolved. Add the pomegranate seeds and

continue to simmer for about half an hour, at which point the liquid should be bright red in color. Strain the mixture through a metal sieve, pressing against the pulp to extract as much of the remaining juices as possible. Allow to cool; add the vodka as a preservative and bottle.

FURTHER READING

If you'd like to read more about the Bacardi Company and its history, I recommend the following book, which provided a lot of the detail that was presented above:

Foster, Peter, *Family Spirits: The Bacardi Saga* (Toronto: Macfarlane Walter & Ross, 1990).

FOR THE RECORD

ESTABLISHING A DIALOGUE among scholars is an invaluable way to ensure that the historical record achieves depth and accuracy even in when it comes to as esoteric a subject as the cocktail. When we first decided to publish this annual journal, we hoped it would prompt discussion on the topics we cover. This section presents communications we receive from readers who have corrections or different insights into previously published articles.

DOWN TO THE SEA IN SHIPS

Philip Duff, Global Brand Ambassador for Bols, wrote us that one of our sources on the Bols company—www. holland.com—was incorrect in the article "Down to the Sea in Ships" (*Mixologist: The Journal of the American Cocktail*, Volume 1). The site stated that Bols was one of 200 jenever houses established in Schiedam, Netherlands. Bols is, and always has been, associated with Amsterdam. In 1575, the Bols family established its distillery in central Rozengracht just outside the city, and remained there until the late 1960s. The company then moved to Nieuw-Vennep (about 8 kilometers outside the city) until the late 1980s, when it moved to a huge facility in Zoetermeer, which is equidistant from Rotterdam, the Hague, and Schiedam.

As Duff explained, the error in this web site's statement probably stems from the fact that Bols purchased some of the most famous distilleries in Schiedam, including Rynbende and Henkes, and that the site's author assumed that since Bols and Ketel dominate the Dutch jenever market, Bols must have had a Schiedam-based distillery at some point in its history.

JOIN US IN CELEBRATING A TRUE AMERICAN ICON!

The Museum of the American COCKTAIL

The Museum of the American Cocktail™ is a nonprofit organization dedicated to providing education in Mixology and preserving the rich history of the American Cocktail. Our exhibit is a fascinating tour of the history of the American cocktail and the way it has influenced music, theater, art, film, and politics around the world during its two hundred year history.

The exhibit at Commander's Palace, Las Vegas, designed by Museum Curator Ted "Dr. Cocktail" Haigh, includes rare books, Prohibition-era literature and music, vintage cocktail shakers, glassware, tools, gadgets, memorabilia, and photographs from the outstanding collections of the founders.

The Museum's New York satellite exhibit, designed by historian Dave Wondrich, focuses on the cocktail's emergence in New York. From the first use of the word "cocktail" in a New York newspaper to the creation of some of the world's most timeless drinks. Film presentations show visitors the great watering holes of old New York, methods for mixing drinks made popular between 1780 and 1920, and how to prepare cocktails that are true New York inventions.

BALANCE

215 West 28 Street New York, NY

and

Commander's Palace

LAS VEGAS
Desert Passage, Aladdin, South Strip

For Information and seminar listings, visit:
www.museumoftheamericancocktail.org

COCKTAIL 200™
May 13, 2006!
www.cocktail200.org

MUSEUM MIXOLOGY SEMINARS

The Museum offers an exciting Mixology Seminar Series given in various cities around the country by influential mixologists and spirits authorities who share their special talents, techniques and stories with participants. Cocktails and hors de oeuvres are served. For a complete list of seminars visit:
www.museumoftheamericancocktail.org

**Help Support the
First Museum in the World
Dedicated to Education in Mixology
and the History of the Cocktail!**

JOIN NOW!

Regular Professional $35/yr.
Online newsletter, chatroom, 15% discount on mixology seminars, museum journal and book purchases.

Gold: Cocktailians; Prof. & Non-Prof. $75/yr.
Online newsletter, chatroom, 20% discount on mixology seminars, museum journal and book purchases..

Industry: Bar, Rest.,Hotel, Retail $150/yr.
Online newsletter, chatroom, 20% discount on mixology seminars, museum journal and book purchases, Free Ad in newsletter.

Enclosed is my check for: $_____

Name: _____

Address: _____

City/State/Zip: _____

Email: _____

Phone: _____

Send to: **MOTAC** P.O. Box 38, Malverne, NY 11565
OR APPLY ONLINE:
www.museumofthe american cocktail.org

Made in the USA